The Wisdom of
MUHAMMAD

The Wisdom of

MUHAMMAD

by
Allama Sir Abdullah
Al-Mamun Al-Suhrawardy

WITH FOREWORD BY
MAHATMA GANDHI

PHILOSOPHICAL
LIBRARY

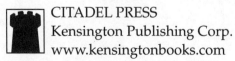

CITADEL PRESS
Kensington Publishing Corp.
www.kensingtonbooks.com

CITADEL PRESS books are published by Kensington Publishing Corp., 850 Third Avenue, New York, NY 10022. Citadel Press and its logo are trademarks of Kensington Publishing Corp.

Titles included in the Wisdom Library are published by arrangement with Philosophical Library.

All Kensington titles, imprints, and distributed lines are available at special quantity discounts for bulk purchases for sales promotions, premiums, fund raising, educational, or institutional use. Special book excerpts or customized printings can also be created to fit specific needs. For details, write or phone the office of the Kensington special sales manager: Kensington Publishing Corp., 850 Third Avenue, New York, NY 10022, attn: Special Sales Department, phone 1-800-221-2647.

First Wisdom Library printing May 2001

10 9 8 7 6 5 4 3 2 1

Printed in the United States of America

Cataloging data for *The Wisdom of Muhammed* may be obtained from the Library of Congress.

ISBN 0-8065-2248-8

لَقَدْ كَانَ لَكُمْ فِي رَسُولِ اللهِ أُسْوَةٌ حَسَنَةٌ *

An excellent pattern have ye in the Messenger of God.—KUR'ĀN, xxxiii. 21.

FOREWORD

I HAVE read Sir Abdullah Suhrawardy's collections of the sayings of the Prophet with much interest and profit. They are among the treasures of mankind, not merely Muslims.

I am a believer in the truth of all the great religions of the world. There will be no lasting peace on earth unless we learn not merely to tolerate but even to respect the other faiths as our own. A reverent study of the sayings of the different teachers of mankind is a step in the direction of such mutual respect.

CALCUTTA.
24 March 1938.

mKGandhi

EDITORIAL NOTE

THE object of the Editor of this series is a very definite one. He desires above all things that these books shall be the ambassadors of goodwill between East and West. He hopes that they will contribute to a fuller knowledge of the great cultural heritage of the East, for only through real understanding will the West be able to appreciate the underlying problems and aspirations of Asia today. He is confident that a deeper knowledge of the great ideals and lofty philosophy of Eastern thought will help to a revival of that true spirit of charity which neither despises nor fears the nations of another creed and colour.

J. L. CRANMER-BYNG
50, ALBEMARLE STREET,
LONDON, W.I.

CONTENTS

Contents

PREFACE

THE compiler and translator of these sayings, Allama Sir Abdullah al-Mamun al-Suhrawardy, Barrister-at-Law, M.A., Ph.D., D.Litt., LL.D., Iftakhar-ul-Milla, Kt., Commander of the Order of Medjedie, was born at Dacca in 1882, and died at Calcutta on the 13th January, 1935. The obituary notice in the London *Times* of 14th January, 1935, gives many details of his life and work, but it does not mention this little book *The Wisdom of Muhammad*, than which none of his works was nearer his heart. There is also no reference to the fact that Abdullah was an extraordinarily brilliant student, winning a number of stipends and scholarships throughout his school and college career. He graduated with honours in Arabic, English and Philosophy, obtaining a first class in his special subjects and standing first of his year both in the B.A. and M.A. examinations of Calcutta University. He was also the first to obtain the Ph.D. degree of the Calcutta University. While studying for the Bar, he took his M.A. degree from the London University, and used to add to his slender allowance from India by lecturing on Arabic letters and jurisprudence, subjects to which he contributed in his later writings and teachings much of value and freshness.

In February 1905, when his *Wisdom of Muhammad* was first published, Abdullah was a young man burning with zeal for Pan-Islamism and dedicating his extraordinary energy and talent to a vision he had of uniting into one cultural and economic, if not political, whole lands which were under Muslim rule, or had a large Muslim population. The Pan-Islamic Society of London, of which he was the founder and first secretary, was at that time an extremely active and vigorous body preaching Islām, converting British and continental Christians, and carrying on intense propaganda for Pan-Islamic unity. The *Wisdom of Muhammad* was one of the Society's publications.

Containing as it does some of the finest Sayings of the Prophet, it attracted the attention of minds widely removed from the ranks of orthodox Islām. It was quoted from in many books and journals, and parts of it were translated into several European languages. An interesting testimony to its success was the correspondence which was initiated after its publication between my late brother and Leo Tolstoy and which continued till the Count's death. He had come to appraise the real personality of the Prophet through this volume, and I am told by a nephew of mine on the authority of one of his daughters whom he had met in Russia that a copy of this book was found in the large overcoat in which he had wrapped himself before setting out on that last walk of his to die in the fields he used to till.

The book had long been out of print, and I had a great deal of difficulty in obtaining it. An old friend of our family [1] sent me his copy from Scotland, and in 1938, with the help of Mr. N. Mukherjee, Proprietor of the Art Press, Calcutta, a reprint was brought out.

For the purpose of the present edition, Professor L. F. Rushbrook Williams, C.B.E., has, at my request, very kindly classified and indexed the 'Sayings' in alphabetical and logical order under various headings, to facilitate reference and comparison. Mr. Mahmood R. Zada, First Secretary of the Royal Legation of Saudi Arabia in London, has compared the 'Sayings' with the original Arabic, and helped me

---

[1] The late Mr. W. R. Gourlay, C.S.I., C.I.E., of Kenbank, Dalry, near Castle Douglas, Scotland.

to translate them into simple English. Out of the 451 'Sayings' in the original publication, we have retranslated 150 and deleted 35 of which we failed to find the original Arabic. I have revised the chapter written by my brother on the Prophet Muhammad, and I have entirely re-written the chapter on Islām, replacing the original very brief sketch.

I earnestly trust that this modest volume will serve in some degree to remove misconceptions as to the meaning and message of our religion, particularly with regard to tolerance in Islām and the status of women.

I would like to express my thanks for the courtesy and help which I have received from Sir John Murray in arranging for the publication of the 'Sayings' in the 'Wisdom of the East Series', and to Mr. Cranmer Byng, the veteran Editor, who has rendered such remarkable service 'as an ambassador of goodwill and understanding between East and West, reviving that true spirit of charity which neither despises nor fears the nations of another creed and colour '.

Any profits which may accrue to me from the sale of this book will be devoted to augment the funds of 'The Servants of Humanity Society', 3 Suhrawardy Avenue, Calcutta.

HASSAN SUHRAWARDY
THE ATHENAEUM,
PALL MALL, LONDON, S.W.I.
January 1941.

The Wisdom of
MUHAMMAD

INTRODUCTION

THE supreme importance of the sayings of Muhammad, apart from their general ethical value, can be fully realised only when one becomes aware that the whole religious, moral, social, and political fabric of a vast section of humanity rests on the Book (the Kur'ān), the sayings and acts (the Sunnah)* of the Prophet, and analogical deductions therefrom.

The Ways and Wont of Muhammad and his utterances form a living commentary on and a supplement to the Kur'ān. Their great importance and their difference from the *obiter dicta* of other teachers lie in this: the utterances of other prophets, sages, and philosophers may become the object of enthusiastic admiration in the absence of any sanction to enforce their translation into practice; whereas the utterances of Muhammad have already acquired the force of law. A Muslim may question the genuineness of an individual saying; but once its authenticity is proved it is as binding upon him as the injunctions and prohibitions in the

See Glossary, page 107.

Kur'ān.* What a powerful influence the example of the Prophet exercises over the hearts and imaginations of his followers may well be realised from the fact that to-day the approved mode of parting the hair and of wearing the beard, and the popularity of the turban and flowing robes in the East, are all due to the conscious or unconscious imitation of that great Teacher who flourished in Arabia at the beginning of the seventh century.

The Table-Talk of the Prophet deals with the most minute and delicate circumstances of life, and the collected body is the Muslim's dictionary of morals and manners. It is therefore not to be wondered at that there are no less than 1,465 collections of the Prophet's sayings extant, of which the more generally used amongst the Sunnis are the 'Six Correct' collections, and those amongst the Shiahs, 'the Four Books'.

This small selection from the authentic utterances of the Prophet cannot claim to be a fair sample of the whole. Perhaps one will miss in this collection the hyperbolical teachings of other Masters, but the ethical sweetness, beauty, strong common sense, practicality, and modernity of thought of some of the utterances will not fail to appeal to higher minds and also strike the attention of lower natures. Some of the sayings are chosen to illustrate the rude and barbarous manners of the people amongst whom the Lawgiver lived, whilst a few are specially meant for the Muslim, the mystic, the spiritualist, and the ṣūfī. If this booklet serves in the least degree to quicken the march of the spirit of Renaissance and Reform now abroad in the Dār-al-Islām, and to awaken an interest in the Faith amongst those Seekers after Truth in the West who are worshippers of the Light and not of the Lamp, the labours of the compiler will be more than amply rewarded.

The Prophet Muhammad

THERE are no historic doubts about the existence of Muhammad; throughout his active career every detail of his life is known. Muhammad was born in Mecca on the 12th Rabi 'I, 20th August in the year 570 of the Christian era. His father, Abdullah, son of Abdul-Muttalib of the clan of Bani Hashim of the tribe of Quraish, died before his birth. According to the custom of the nobility of the Quraish, the child when only eight days old was handed to a Bedouin nurse called Haleema from the tribe of Bani Sa'd, to be brought up by her in the healthy atmosphere of the desert. At the age of five, Muhammad returned to the care of his mother, Amina, the daughter of Wahb, the Chief of the clan of Bani Zuhra, but she died a year later. His grandfather, Abdul-Muttalib, the Chief of Bani Hashim and the leader of the Meccans, in whose loving care he was, died when he was eight and Muhammad was brought up by his uncle Abū Ṭālib, who was to prove his shield and protector when some thirty years later his preaching brought upon him the enmity of the Meccans. Abū Ṭālib was a merchant of modest means, and when Muhammad grew up he assisted his uncle in his business. At the age of 12, he accompanied his uncle in a merchant's caravan to Syria. To the young, vigorous and fresh mind of Muhammad, who had no school learning, the glimpses into the contrasts and similarities of the beliefs, customs and civilisations of diverse countries and peoples must have opened up glorious vistas and left lasting impressions. Later, Abū Ṭālib's business began to dwindle and Muhammad earned his living as a shepherd. Thoughtful by nature, this occupation gave him full scope to contemplate the universe and commune with the creation.

Arabia at this time was in a state of religious chaos and political dissolution. The Arabs were steeped in ignorance and perpetually at war with one another; they were mostly nomadic except for those tribes living in the few cities scattered through the land, the Holy City of Mecca being inhabited by the different clans of the tribe of Quraish. Apart from a few Jewish settlements in the northwest, a few Christian tribes on the Syrian border and in the extreme southwest, and a few individuals known as Haneefs who held a monotheistic faith, the whole population of Arabia worshipped idols, stars, stones and fetishes. The idolatry of his people, their immorality, and the terrible treatment of the poor and the weak set Muhammad's mind and soul aflame with intense horror and righteous disgust. In the solitude of the desert and hills where he tended his sheep Muhammad reflected on all these questions. He had now reached the age of twenty-one, and had conducted himself with such rectitude and nobility of character that he was called 'Al-Ameen' or the Trusty. The war of the Fijar, which was started by the murder of a member of the Hawazin tribe, and lasted for four years, made the leaders of the Meccans reflect on the dire results which lawlessness had brought upon them. Muhammad and the other leading members of his clan Bani Hashim and their relations Bani Al-Muttalib and the leaders of the clans of Bani Zuhra and Bani Taym formed themselves into a league pledged to defend the weak and champion the oppressed, freeman and slave alike, and to vindicate their rights against tyranny and aggression. This league, known as *Hilf Al-Fudhool*, exercised such efficient protection that for a long time the mere threat of its intervention was sufficient to repress lawlessness and afford redress to the helpless. Muhammad was very proud of his membership in this chivalrous league, and used to say: "I would not have the riches of the earth in exchange for my membership of it."

Muhammad was content with his lot as a shepherd, but his uncle, Abū Ṭālib, desired something better for him, and obtained him employment with a rich widow, Khadija, the daughter of Khuweilid, son of Asad, and thus Muhammad found himself at the age of 25 in charge of a caravan conveying merchandise to Syria. On Muhammad's return, Khadija was so pleased with his successful management of her business, and was so attracted by his nobility of character, reports about which she heard from her old servant who had accompanied him, that she sent her sister to offer the young man her hand. Muhammad had felt drawn to Khadija, and so matters were soon arranged and, though Khadija was by fifteen years his senior, their twenty-six years of married life were singularly happy. Muhammad continued to work as a merchant, and his fair dealings further enhanced his reputation as *Al-Ameen* the Trusty. In the year 605 of the Christian era, a dispute arose during the reconstruction of the *Ka'aba* which threatened to plunge the different clans of the Quraish into war, but the sagacious arbitration of Muhammad saved the situation and settled the dispute to everyone's satisfaction. He continued to take an ever-increasing interest in public affairs and to exert himself in the service of the poor, the helpless and the weak. Many were the slaves who owed their freedom to Muhammad, and many were the widows and orphans who lived on his generosity. When Khadija made a gift to him of a slave called Zaid, who had been presented to her by her nephew, he immediately set the slave lad free. Though he was now a free man, Zaid insisted on remaining in Muhammad's household as his personal servant, and Muhammad rewarded his devotion by adopting him as his son.

Whenever the iniquities of his people oppressed him, Muhammad retired to the solitude of a cave in Mount Hira outside Mecca. There his soul, 'soaring aloft, tried to peer into the mysteries of creation, of life and death, of good and evil, to find order out of chaos.' Solitude became a passion with him, and every year he would retire to the cave in Mount Hira for the whole month of Ramadan, to meditate and commune with the Invisible Power which fills the Universe. It was on one of these occasions, when he was forty years of age, that Muhammad received the call. Professor Max Muller says: 'The Father of Truth chooses His own prophets, and He speaks to them in a voice stronger than the voice of thunder.' One night, in the solitude of the cave, whilst lying absorbed in his thoughts, Muhammad was commanded by a mighty Voice to go forth and preach. Twice the Voice called and twice he ignored the call. "Preach," called the Voice for the third time, and an answer was wrung out of Muhammad's heart and he said, "What shall I preach?" "Preach in the name of thy Lord!" replied the Voice. This, the first revelation, is contained in the short 96th Sura of the Kur'ān: 'When the Voice had ceased to speak, telling him how from the minutest beginnings man had been called into existence and lifted up by understanding and knowledge of the Lord, who is most beneficent, and who by the pen revealed that which men did not know, Muhammad woke from his trance and felt as if the words spoken to his soul had been written on his heart.'

Alarmed by his experience, Muhammad rose trembling, and hastened home to seek rest and solace for his troubled mind and tortured soul in Khadija's tender care, and she calmed and comforted him. When he had recovered sufficiently, he sought the solitude of the hills to soothe his anguish of mind when the Angel of God appeared to him and recalled him to his duty to mankind. Awestricken, he hurried back into his house and asked to be wrapped in warm garments. Khadija did her best to reassure him, saying that his conduct through life had been such that God would not let a harmful spirit come to him. She consulted her kinsman, Waraqa son of Naufal, an old man of over 90 years who knew the Scriptures of the Jews and the Christians, and he declared that the heavenly message which came to Moses of old had come to Muhammad, and that he was chosen as a Prophet of God. The very thought of being chosen out of all mankind with such a Mission profoundly disturbed Muhammad's humble and devout mind. Khadija his wife was the first to accept the truth of his Mission, and he then communicated his experiences to his cousin Ali, his adopted son Zaid, and his intimate friend Abu Bakr; these persons, who knew him best and had lived and worked with him and noted all his movements, and the sincerity of his character, became his first converts. For a year or two Muhammad preached among his immediate friends and relatives, and made several converts, but the Meccans as a whole regarded him with indifference as one who had become a little mad. Struggling in his mind with doubts as to the divinity of his Mission, and in a state of great depression, Muhammad was lying covered up in blankets when he heard the Divine Voice calling upon him to arise and preach. 'O thou wrapped up in thy mantle, arise and warn!' (Kur'ān lxxiv.). Conviction now replaced doubt, and Muhammad arose and girded himself for the work to which he had been called. Standing alone, he proclaimed the glory of God, publicly denounced the idolatry of his people and their evil ways, and called them to God and the better life (Kur'ān lxxxi. 19–28).

The Quraish were the guardians of the *Ka'aba*, the holy

place to which all Arabia made pilgrimage, and it was a source of great prestige and profit to their city, Mecca. They were therefore seriously alarmed and assumed active hostility towards Muhammad, who was now publicly preaching against the worship of the idols in the *Ka'aba*, which ranked first among their vested interests. At the season of the pilgrimage, men were posted on all the roads to warn the tribes against the madman who was preaching against their gods. The early converts of Muhammad, who were mostly humble folk, were subjected to great oppression, and in spite of his rank, Muhammad himself would have been killed if the Quraish had not been deterred by the fear of blood vengeance from his powerful clan, the Bani Hashim. The Meccans' persecution waxed higher as Muhammad's converts increased in number and influence. They tried a compromise, offering to accept Muhammad's religion if he would agree to their idols being worshipped as intercessors to the God of Muhammad. When this negotiation failed, a deputation was sent to Muhammad's uncle, Abū Ṭālib, offering Muhammad riches and power as an inducement to stop preaching, and threatening that unless he did so Abū Ṭālib would bear the consequences with him. Muhammad was informed of what had happened, and his uncle begged him to cease his attempts to convert the Meccans, and thus put an end to constant trouble. Muhammad said: "Though they gave me the sun in my right hand and the moon in my left to turn me back from my undertaking, yet will I not pause till the Lord carry His cause to victory, or till I die for it." Muhammad turned away to leave, but his uncle said to him, "Go in peace, son of my brother, and say what thou wilt, for I will on no condition abandon thee." This attempt having failed, the Meccans sent 'Otba Ibn Rabi'a to Muhammad direct. "Dear kinsman," said 'Otba, "thou art distinguished by thy qualities and thy descent. But now thou hast sown division among our people and created dissension in our families; thou denouncest our gods and goddesses, thou dost tax our ancestors with impiety. We have a proposition to make to thee. Think well before refusing it. If thou wishest to acquire riches by this affair, we will collect for thee a fortune larger than is possessed by any of us; if thou desirest honour and dignity, we shall make thee our Chief and we shall not do a thing without thee; if thou desirest dominion we shall make thee our King." Muhammad recited a portion from the Kur'ān proclaiming the glory of God, denouncing the wickedness of idolatry and calling on mankind to worship God alone and lead a good life. Then he said to 'Otba: "Thou hast heard."

The Meccans' fury now knew no bounds. Muhammad, the respected citizen of rank and high descent, the *Al-Ameen* of his people, was henceforth subjected to insults, to personal violence, and to the bitterest persecution, and his converts were most relentlessly oppressed. Feeling deeply grieved at the sad plight of his followers, Muhammad advised them in the fifth year of his Mission (615 of the Christian era) to leave the country and seek refuge from the persecution of the idolaters among the Christian people of Abyssinia. Muhammad and a few stalwart followers remained in Mecca and suffered untold misery and oppression, but still their number continued to increase. The Quraish, in their exasperation, outlawed Muhammad, and asked his clan to forgo their right of avenging his blood. Though unbelievers, and participators in the persecution, the proud clansmen refused to give up this right at the bidding of the Meccans, who thereupon boycotted them. Muhammad, the small band of his followers, and Bani

Hashim and Bani Al-Muttalib, suffered such terrible hardships that the better minds among the Meccans grew weary of the social ostracism of old friends and neighbours, and, after three years, towards the end of 619 of the Christian era, the ban was lifted. The Bani Hashim and Bani Al-Muttalib were now free to follow their vocations, but opposition to Muhammad became ever more implacable.

A year later, Muhammad lost his uncle and protector, the noble Abū Ṭālib, and his beloved wife, the good Khadija, in whose love and devotion he had found comfort, solace and encouragement. The death of Abū Ṭālib removed the last check on the Meccans' violence. Defenceless, in continual peril of his life, more than once it seemed all over with Muhammad, more than once his life turned on a straw. Persecution grew fiercer and fiercer, and Muhammad, seeking refuge in the neighbouring city of Taif, met with great hostility and barely escaped with his life. But a turning point in his career was at hand. In a party of pilgrims from the prosperous city of Yathrib, Muhammad made several converts. After the Pilgrimage, the men of Yathrib returned to their city with a Muslim teacher, and in the following year, at the time of pilgrimage, seventy-three Muslims from Yathrib came to Mecca to vow allegiance to the Prophet and invited him to go to their city. Muhammad took council with his Meccan followers, and it was decided that they should emigrate to Yathrib. They left gradually and unobtrusively, Muhammad remaining to the last. Their departure was soon discovered by the Quraish, who decided to slay Muhammad before he too could escape; for although they hated the idea of Muhammad preaching in their midst, they dreaded still more the spread of his influence if he escaped from Mecca. The Meccans therefore cast lots, and chose forty men, one from each clan; who took a solemn vow to kill Muhammad; they were to strike simultaneously so that the murder could not be avenged by blood feud on any one clan; but on the night they were to kill him, Muhammad, with Abu Bakr, left Mecca and, eluding his pursuers over 200 miles of desert and rocks, he reached Yathrib on Friday the 4th of Rabi 'I, the 2nd July, 622. This event is called the Hijra (Hegira) or emigration. It marks the greatest crisis in the history of Muhammad's Mission, and the Muslim calendar is named after it (vide Glossary, page 107).

Muhammad was now free to preach, and his followers increased rapidly; but the Meccans, who had sent an embassy to distant Abyssinia demanding the extradition of the Muslims who had sought refuge there, were not going to allow Muhammad's movement to take root in Yathrib, henceforth to be known as Medina (short for Medinat-ul-Nabi, the City of the Prophet). They organised three great expeditions against the city, but all were beaten back. It was not until the eighth year after the Hijra that the Muslims were able to put an end to this war by gaining a bloodless victory over Mecca. The Meccans, who had relentlessly oppressed Muhammad and his followers for twenty-one years, expected dire vengeance, but in the hour of their defeat they were treated with the greatest magnanimity. "Go, you are free!" were the words in which Muhammad gave them general amnesty. The Prophet removed all the idols which were in the Ka'aba, saying, "Truth hath come, darkness hath vanished away" (Kur'ān xvii. 81), and the Muslim call to prayer was heard in this ancient sanctuary. The surrender of Mecca was followed by the submission of the surrounding tribes, and the acknowledgement of Muhammad's spiritual and temporal leadership over the whole of Arabia.

During the 9th year of the Hijra, deputations came from

all parts of Arabia to swear allegiance to the Prophet, and to hear the Kur'ān. Islam now spread by leaps and bounds, and the conversion of the Arabs was complete. In the 10th year, Muhammad went to Mecca as a pilgrim, and he felt it was for the last time because of the Revelations which he received (cx. and v. 4). On his return to Medina, he fell ill of a mortal fever. It lasted for fifteen days, but he continued to lead the prayers until three days before his death, when he deputised Abu Bakr. At early dawn on the last day of his earthly life, Muhammad came out from his room beside the mosque and joined the public prayers, but later in the day he died. The end came peacefully; murmuring of pardon and the company of the righteous in Paradise, the preacher of Islam breathed his last, at the age of 63 on Wednesday the 12th Rabi 'I in the 11th year after the Hijra (633 of the Christian era).

Non-Muslim writers have paid the following tributes to the character of Muhammad:

'His moral teachings sprang from a pure and exalted mind aflame with religious enthusiasm. From being a persecuted preacher exiled to Medina, he rose to political power. This he enjoyed only in the last few years of his life, and this he used for the spiritual and material welfare of Muslims.

'Such indeed was the munificence of his good works that he died in debt, some of his belongings in pawn with a Jew—among them his only shield for which he obtained three measures of meal.

'He lived in great humility, performing the most menial tasks with his own hands; he kindled the fire, swept the floor, milked the ewes, patched his own garments and cobbled his own shoes.

'He laboured for the amelioration of the slaves' lot, liberating any that were presented to him.'—BERTRAM THOMAS.

'He who, standing alone, braved for years the hatred of his people is the same who was never the first to withdraw his hand from another's clasp; the beloved of children, who never passed a group of little ones without a smile from his wonderful eyes and a kind word for them, sounding all the kinder in that sweet-toned voice. . . . He was one of those happy few who have attained the supreme joy of making one great truth their very life-spring. He was the messenger of the one God; and never to his life's end did he forget who he was, or the message which was the marrow of his being. He brought his tidings to his people with a grand dignity sprung from the consciousness of his high office, together with a most sweet humility whose roots lay in the knowledge of his own weakness.'—STANLEY LANE-POOLE.

'His humanity extended itself to the lower creation. He forbade the employment of living birds as targets for marksmen and remonstrated with those who ill-treated their camels. . . . Foolish acts of cruelty which were connected with old superstitions were swept away by him. . . . No more was a dead man's camel to be tied to his tomb to perish of thirst and hunger. No more was the evil eye to be propitiated by the bleeding of a certain proportion of the herd. No more was the rain to be conjured by tying burning torches to the tails of oxen. . . . The manes and tails of horses were not to be cut . . . nor were asses to be branded.' —D. S. MARGOLIOUTH.

'Sleeping one day under a palm-tree, Muhammad awoke suddenly to find an enemy named Du'thur standing over him with drawn sword. "O Muhammad, who is there now to save thee?" cried the man. "God!" answered Muhammad. Du'thur, while trying to strike, stumbled and dropped his sword. Muhammad seized it and cried in turn: "O Du'thur, who is there now to save thee?" "No one," replied Du'thur. "Then learn to be merciful," said Muhammad, and handed him back his weapon. Du'thur became one of his firmest friends.'—GORHAM'S *Ethics of the Great Religions.*

Islām

The soul of Islām is its declaration of the unity of God; its heart is the inculcation of an absolute resignation to His will.

EDWIN ARNOLD.

THE religion preached by Muhammad has been called *Mahommedanism,* and its followers Mahommedans, as parallel terms to Christianity and Christians. These are misnomers. Its correct name is Islām, and the followers of the faith of Islām are called Muslims. The word '*Islām*' means 'absolute submission to the Will of God', but this does not imply any idea of fatalism any more than 'Thy will be done' does to the Christian. In its ethical sense it signifies 'Striving after the Ideal (Righteousness)'. 'Islām' is derived from a root word which means 'peace'. The greeting of the Muslims is 'Assalam o-Aleikum', which means 'Peace be unto you'.

Muslims do not worship *Muhammad,* who, according to their religion, was a Prophet divinely inspired, but a mortal man. 'Muhammad is only (a man) charged with a *Mission,* before whom there have been others who received heavenly Missions and died.'[1]*

Muhammad did not claim to be the founder of a new religion; his mission was to restore the earlier religions to their pristine purity.[2] The Muslim believes in a chain of inspired prophets [3] and teachers, who taught the same truths,

* For this and other numbered references, see pp. 113ff.

beginning with the dawn of religious consciousness in man. With the evolution, progress, and advancement of humanity, the Divine Will reveals and manifests itself more clearly and distinctly. They believe in the Divine Revelations[4] of all earlier prophets, and that the Kur'ān *is* the latest Revelation of them all, and has been sent to revive and consolidate the fundamental truths of religion, to the end that it might continue in the earth.[5]

The Kur'ān makes no distinction between any of the prophets,[6] and the Muslims use for all of them the same term of respect, 'Sayedana, Hazrat' (My Lord and Master), as they use for their own prophet, Muhammad.

The Muslim believes in the message of Lord Jesus but not in his divinity or sonship.[7] 'We are all of God, and towards Him are we progressing.' [8] The spark of the Divine is latent in the heart of every atom.

The Muslim conception of God is that He does not assume human form and is free from all human needs and imperfections; He is One, Invisible, Eternal, Indivisible, Beneficent, Almighty, All-Knowing, Omnipresent, Just, Merciful, Loving and Forgiving.[9] Belief in the unity of God is the essential requirement for a Muslim; no baptism or formal ceremony of conversion is necessary as in the Christian religion.

The Muslims believe that the Jews made the mistake of denying the Mission of Christ, and that the Christians erred by exceeding the bounds of praise and deifying Christ. In order to avoid any misconception, Muhammad's position as a Messenger or Prophet of God is repeatedly made clear. (Saying 57, page 46.)

There is *no monasticism nor any priesthood in Islām*. Muhammad said: "The retirement that becometh my followers is to live in the world and yet to sit in the corner of a

Mosque in the expectation of prayers." Muslims do not believe that any priest, pastor or saint can intervene or medi-
ate between the individual worshipper and his Creator, nor
can anyone grant indulgence or absolution from sins. In
congregational worship any Muslim of good character can
be the 'Imam' or leader of the prayers in the Mosque. The
idea of a church and clergy in the Christian sense is foreign
to and unknown in Islām.

The Muslims believe in the immortality of the soul, and
the accountability for human actions in another existence;
but they do not accept the doctrine of original sin, and
hence, according to Islām, the souls of unbaptised babes are
not lost. Muslims do not believe in the doctrine of Redemption or of vicarious atonement: each soul must work
out its own salvation. It is therefore held that, provided a
person believes in the cardinal doctrines of Islām, no one
can say that he is not a Muslim. If a bad Muslim amends
and reforms by sincere repentance, God will forgive his
sins.[10] Islām does not promise salvation to Muslims alone,
but gives equal hope to the righteous and God-fearing of all
religions. 'Whether Muslim, Jew, Christian or Sabian, whosoever believes in God and in the Last Day and does good
to others, verily he shall find his recompense with his Lord.
For him there shall be no terror, neither any torment or suffering.'[11]

TOLERATION

Islām is against aggression; sanction is given for war only
in self-defence. 'Fight in the way of God against those who
attack you, but begin not hostilities. Verily, God loveth not
the aggressors.'[12] 'And if they (enemies) incline towards
peace, incline thou also to it, and trust in God.'[13]

There is no ground for the oft-repeated allegation that Islām is intolerant and was propagated by the sword. The Kur'ān states clearly 'there is no compulsion in religion.'[14] It was only when her liberty and particularly her right of freedom of worship was threatened that 'Islām seized the sword in self-defence, and held it in self-defence, as it will ever do. But Islām never interfered with the dogmas of any moral faith. It never invented the rack or the stake for stifling difference of opinion, or strangling the human conscience, or exterminating heresy.' . . . 'It has been alleged that a warlike spirit was infused into mediaeval Christianity by aggressive Islām! The massacres of Justinian and the fearful wars of Christian Clovis in the name of religion occurred long before the time of Muhammad.'* The conduct of the Christian Crusaders when they captured Jerusalem provides a striking contrast to the behaviour of the Muslims when they occupied the city 600 years earlier.

'When the Khalif Omar took Jerusalem, A.D. 637, he rode into the city by the side of the Patriarch Sophronius, conversing with him on its antiquities. At the hour of prayer, he declined to perform his devotions in the Church of the Resurrection, in which he chanced to be, but prayed on the steps of the Church of Constantine†; 'for', said he to the Patriarch, 'had I done so, the Mussulmans in a future age might have infringed the treaty, under colour of imitating my example.' But in the capture by the Crusaders, the brains of young children were dashed out against the walls; infants were pitched over the battlements; men were roasted

---

* The Rt. Honble. Syed Ameer Ali, P.C., C.I.E., M.A., D.L., LL.D., ex-Judge Calcutta High Court, in his *The Spirit of Islām* (1891), pages 311, 314.

† As a matter of fact, it was in the street.—[ED.]

at fires; some were ripped up, to see if they had swallowed gold; the Jews were driven into their synagogue and there burnt; a massacre of nearly 70,000 persons took place, and the Pope's legate were seen partaking in the triumph!'*

According to the Muslim Laws of War, those of the conquered peoples who embraced Islām became the equals of the conquerors in all respects; and those who chose to keep their own religion had to pay a tribute (called *jizyah*), but after that enjoyed full liberty of conscience, and were secured and protected in their occupations.[15] In civil employment they could even become Ministers of State. Non-Muslims serving in the army were exempted from payment of this tax, and could even hold high command.

The *jizyah* has been much misrepresented: it was not, as is usually stated, a tax on non-Muslims as a penalty for refusal to accept the faith of Islām; it was paid in return for the protection given to them by the Muslim army, to which they were not compulsorily conscripted like the Muslims. Non-Muslims were exempt from payment of *zakat*, the poor-rate of 2½ percent on one's total assets for each year, which was compulsory for Muslims, and the *jizyah* tax which they did have to pay was very light: the rich paid 48 *dirhams* a year (a *dirham* is about 5d.), the middle class paid 24, while from the field-labourers and artisans only 12 *dirhams* were taken. The tax could be paid in kind; cattle, merchandise, household effects, even needles were accepted in lieu of specie, but not pigs, wine, or dead animals. The tax was levied only on able-bodied men, and not on women and children; the aged and the indigent, the blind and the maimed were specially exempt, as were the priests and monks, unless they were well-to-do (Bell, pp. xxv, 173,

* Draper, *History of the Intellectual Development of Europe*, vol. ii, p. 22.

and Abu Yusuf, pp. 69–71, quoted by Sir Thomas Arnold in *The Preaching of Islām*, p. 60).

When the Roman Emperor embraced Christianity, the population of the whole Roman Empire, including Egypt, was by decree forced to renounce all other religions and adopt Christianity; but it was not until after five hundred years of Muslim rule in Egypt that, as the result of peaceful conversion, the Muslims formed even 50 percent of the total population. In Northern India (the United Provinces of Agra and Oudh), which has been under Muslim rule for six centuries, and in which are situated the important Muslim capital cities of Agra, Delhi, Lucknow, Allahabad and Rampur, there is a Hindu population of 41 million, against the Muslim population of 7 million, according to the Census of 1931. The Hindus and Muslims have lived together as fellow citizens for centuries, and their reciprocal social and cultural influences have created a fusion which can be seen in their similarity of language, dress, and general level of culture. The Hindus in these parts are nearer to the Muslims in all these respects and provide a striking contrast to their Hindu brethren of the same castes living in southern India.

SOCIAL REFORMS: POSITION OF WOMEN

Islām forbids drinking, gambling, usury and all forms of vice. It introduced far-reaching changes in the social structure of the period: Muhammad said, "Henceforth, usury is prohibited. The debtor shall return only the principal; and the beginning will be made with the loans of my uncle Abbas, son of Abdul-Muttalib," and "Henceforth the vengeance of blood is forbidden and all blood feuds abolished commencing with the murder of my cousin Ibn Rabi'a, son of Al-Harith son of Abdul-Muttalib."*

So far back as the seventh century of the Christian era, Islām abolished the horrible practice of female infanticide prevalent among the pagan Arabs,[16] gave clear directions leading to the restriction of polygamy,†[17] restrained the unlimited rights exercised by men over their wives, and gave woman both spiritual and material equality with man.[18] Muslim women inherit a share of the property of their husbands, parents and kinsfolk.[19] Pierre Crabites, an American judge in the Cairo mixed tribunals, after a long experience of Muslim law as administered in the Egyptian capital, says: 'Muhammad was probably the greatest champion of women's rights the world has ever seen. Islām conferred upon the Muslim wife property rights and juridical status exactly the same as that of her husband. She is free to dispose of and manage her financial assets as she pleases, without let or hindrance from her husband.' [20]

Bertram Thomas says: 'His humanity was all-embracing. He never ceased to champion the cause of woman against the ill-treatment of his contemporaries. He condemned the practice of inheriting the widow with the rest of an estate as though she were a chattel.‡ She must not be a despised creature to be ashamed of and to be ill treated any more, but a person to love and cherish and respect: at her feet lay the gates of paradise.'

And so with slavery: he laboured for the amelioration of

* Sermon on Mount Arafat, during his Farewell Pilgrimage in the 10th year of the Hijra.

† The Kur'ān is the first amongst the sacred books to put a restriction on polygamy by religious enactment.

‡ The Jewish laws of inheriting a brother's childless widow and of divorcing a childless wife were also made illegal by Muhammad.

the slaves' lot, liberating any that were presented to him. He taught that the slave mother should not be separated from her children, extolled the freeing of slaves as penance, lauded the feeding of the orphan in times of famine and the poor man who lies in the dust. Islām laid the foundation for the abolition of slavery by making the manumission of captives of war an item of expenditure in the budget of the Muslim State. In any case, slavery as understood in the West is unknown to the Muslims—the Memluk Sultans of Egypt, the slave kings and Malliks of Indian history are examples to prove this point.

Great social changes were brought about by breaking down the differences between free-man and freed-man; placing every Muslim under the protection of the entire community, and instituting a compulsory poor-rate *(zakat)* by which every Muslim had to pay 2½ percent of his total assets for the year to be collected in a central Treasury and distributed among the poor.

EQUALITY AND FRATERNITY

Islām teaches that all men are equal before God. There is no colour or race prejudice, and no distinction between Arab and non-Arab—goodness is the only criterion of worth. Muslims are spread all over the world and in many countries form the majority of the population. Though so widely separated by land and sea, and in spite of the diversity of race, nationality and colour, a living spirit of brotherhood, whose loyalties outweigh those of either kin or tribe, binds together the followers of the faith of Islām to-day just as it did when the first followers of the Prophet of Arabia embraced the religion.

The Muslims are not broken up by caste restrictions based on occupation or wealth, or by barriers against inter-marriage. The Haj is not a pilgrimage in the ordinary sense. It is not a visit to a place of sanctity to which miracles and superstitions are attached. It is a commemoration of a great event in the spiritual life of Abraham. It is a symbol of the journey of life, and an annual re-enactment of the principles of equality and brotherhood. There, the rich and the poor alike appear in the congregation for worship and in the sacred precincts of the Ka'aba clad in a simple unembroidered, unstitched, white garment, with bare head and either bare-foot or with an unstitched sandal; the women keep their heads covered but their faces unveiled. Here, as in any place of worship throughout the Muslim world, the prince and the peasant pray together in the same room, and indeed can sit in the same ranks. No one has any right of precedence in the House of God.

The ethics of Islām will be apparent from the following quotation from the Kur'ān: 'It is not righteousness that ye turn your faces (in prayer) to the East and the West; but righteous is he who believes in God and in the Day of Judgement, in all the Scriptures and in all the Prophets; and gives of his wealth, in spite of his love for it, to kinfolk, to orphans, to the needy and to the wayfarer, and for the ransom of captives of war and to set slaves free, and who pays the poor-rate (*zakat*) and keeps his promise and treaty when he makes one, and the patient in tribulation and adversity and in time of stress. Such are they who are sincere. Such are the God-fearing.'[21]

The obligatory duties for the Muslims are the following:

1. Affirmation of belief in the unity of God and the recognition of the Divine Mission of Muhammad as a Messenger of God (cardinal doctrines of Islām).

2. Prayers five times a day.*

3. Fasting for one month in every lunar year.†

4. Obligatory annual payment of *zakat* or poor-rate, for the relief of the needy (one-fortieth, 2½ percent of the value of a person's movable possessions for the year).

5. Pilgrimage to Mecca at least once in a person's lifetime. Incumbent on those whose financial, mental and physical conditions, and family obligations, permit it.

MUSLIM PRAYERS

As has already been pointed out, the Muslims are required to pray five times a day, but as the prayers are short and to the point, they do not take up much time nor weary the mind. In fact, they help to discipline the mind and develop its capacity for concentration, by lifting up the heart to God and feeling the comfort and strength of His presence. Of the five periods allotted for prayers, none can be called irrational. Nor can the midday prayers be criticised as interfering with the exigencies of modern business practice, for it must not be forgotten that in the middle of the day there is always an interruption of work for the midday

---

* (1) Dawn or sunrise; (2) midday; (3) mid-afternoon; (4) sunset; (5) evening, before retiring (*see* Appendix, page 116).

The Muslims perform congregational worship with a sermon in a Mosque at noon on Fridays, corresponding to the Saturday of the Jews and the Sunday of the Christians; also twice annually in the forenoon, during the 'Id-al-Fitr and the Id-al-Adha.

† Subjugation of the passions and fasting of the senses. During fasts a Muslim must abstain from vain talk, disputes and luxuries. He is not allowed to eat, drink or smoke between dawn and sunset. The infirm and those who are not physically fit, or are on a journey, are excused, but must feed the indigent, and carry out the obligation when fit and able to do so.

meal, which is a physical necessity, and during this interval a Muslim can easily find a few minutes in which to say his prayers, thus satisfying his spiritual needs, and resuming his work refreshed and fortified both in body and in mind. Besides this, the Muslim law provides that if, for any special reasons, the prayers cannot be said within the prescribed period, it is permissible to offer them at the earliest opportunity.

The form of Muslim prayers described in the Appendix is based on the traditions of the practices of the Prophet, and was prescribed to maintain a uniformity of practice. The Muslim is not required to put on any special vestments; there is no music or incense nor any such rituals as are considered necessary for communal worship in other religions. Islām does not require any ceremony of consecration of the ground on which the Muslim builds his place of worship (*musjid*, mosque), nor does the Kur'ān recognise such a place as essential for the due worship of God. 'It is one of the glories of Islām', says an English writer,* 'that its temples are not made with hands, and that its ceremonies can be performed anywhere upon God's earth or under his heaven.' The Muslim offers his prayers wherever he happens to be at the appointed hour—he can pray standing, sitting or lying down; alone, or in company. For the soldier, it is enough if he whispers a remembrance in the recesses of his heart amid the heat and clamour of the battlefield. Every man and woman learns to say the prayers individually or in groups 'with a mind not befogged but able to understand all that is said' (iv. 43).

The Muslims believe that, while praying, they are in the

* Sir William Hunter (Bengal Civil Service), *Our Indian Mussulmans*, (1871), page 179.

presence of their Maker, and therefore stand in orderly rows, and pray in a respectful attitude. They turn their faces towards Mecca (the *Ka'aba*), not to worship anything or anyone, but as the central point round which, at the appointed hours of prayer, are focused the religious thoughts of Muslims all the world over, and each feels that he is one of the great community which keeps alive the memory of the inviolable place of worship where Abraham prayed to one God without partner or associate, and which again saw the light of the regenerated truth preached by Muhammad. The Kur'ān does not teach that God is to be found in any particular direction: 'Unto God belongeth the East and the West, and whithersoever ye turn, there is the presence of thy Lord. Behold, God is All-Pervading, All-Knowing' (ii. 115).

Islām makes cleanliness a part of godliness.[22] Prayers cannot be offered in a state of impurity (iv. 43). The worshipper must be clean in mind as well as in body, and wear a clean, simple and decent dress. The parts most likely to be soiled—the hands, feet and face—are washed before prayers in the prescribed manner, and this is considered sufficient before daily prayers, but for the congregational prayers on Fridays and on 'Id days, a complete bath and change of garments are necessary. Before attending public worship one is also directed not to smoke, eat or drink anything that may make one's breath a nuisance to fellow-worshippers. These are excellent hygienic rules, and help one to achieve the essential requirement of cleansing the mind and heart from worldly thoughts.

POLYGAMY

With regard to polygamy, Muhammad did not introduce this practice, as has so often been wrongly alleged. The Scriptures and the other sacred books bear abundant proof of the fact that it was recognised as lawful and, indeed, widely practised by patriarchal prophets, Zoroastrians, Hindus, and Jews. In Arabia and all the surrounding countries a system of temporary marriages, marriages of convenience, and unrestricted concubinage was also prevalent; this, together with polygamy, had most disastrous effects on the entire social and moral structure, which Muhammad remedied.

Muhammad married Khadija at the age of 25, and he took no other wife during the twenty-six years of their married life. He married 'Āishah, daughter of Abu Bakr, at the age of 54, three years after the death of Khadija. After this marriage, he took other wives, about whom non-Muslim writers have directed much unjust criticism against him. The facts are that all these ladies were old maids or widows left destitute and without protection during the repeated wars of persecution, and as head of the State at Medina the only proper way, according to the Arab code, in which Muhammad could extend both protection and maintenance to them was by marriage. The only young person was Maria the Copt, who was presented to him as a captive of war, and whom he immediately liberated, but she refused to leave his kind protection and he therefore married her.

'History proves conclusively that, until very recent times, polygamy was not considered to be so reprehensible as it is now. St. Augustine himself seems to have observed in it no intrinsic immorality or sinfulness, and declared that polygamy was not a crime where it was the legal institution of a country. The German reformers, as Hallam points out, even so late as the sixteenth century, admitted the validity of a second or third marriage contemporaneously with the first, in default of issue and other similar causes.'

Polygamy was consequential upon the social necessities

of the age and moral conceptions of the people of the time: (1) To ensure an increase in the birthrate and thereby the chance of replacing the depleted male population due to constant intertribal warfare. (2) Women were so helpless that marriage gave them a means of obtaining both bread and protection, and it was a chivalrous act to marry as many women as they could support. (3) It was considered a great indignity on the family, indeed on the whole clan, if a girl remained unmarried, or married below her social status. Eligible bridegrooms not only had more than one offer of marriage, but parents vied with each other in providing inducements in the form of valuable jewellery and property as dowers.

In later times polygamy became a self-indulgent vice. It is to the credit of Islām that in the 4th year of the Muslim era, that is about 1,356 years ago, not only did the law relieve parents from the necessity of providing burdensome dowers, but on the contrary made it incumbent on the husband to fix a suitable dower *(maher)* on his wife at the time of marriage, and put a clear restriction on polygamy by religious enactment. 'Ye may marry of the women who seem good to you, two or three or four, but if ye fear that ye cannot observe equity between them, then espouse but a single wife' (iv. 3). Some Muslims contend that the unrestricted number of wives allowed in pre-Islāmic times has been limited by the above verse of the Kur'ān to a maximum of four, provided one is able to treat them with perfect equality. They therefore divide material things equally between their wives, and also equally apportion the hours they spend in their company, and thus think that they are not breaking the law. On the other hand, the growing majority of Muslims interpret the above verse as a clear direction towards monogamy, and it has become customary among all classes of the Indian Muslims to insert in the marriage-deed *(Kabin-nama)* a clause by which the intending husband formally undertakes not to take another wife during the continuance of the first marriage. Verse 129 of chapter iv declares : 'And ye will never be able to be equitable and just between women, no matter how much ye may strive to do so.' Reading this verse together with verse 3 of chapter iv, given above, and considering the fact that it is impossible to show equality of affection to one's children, let alone to one's wives, there can be no doubt that the direction is clearly towards monogamy.

The feeling against polygamy has become a strong social force amongst Indian Muslims, and the most progressive Muslim countries have already authoritatively declared polygamy, like slavery and the seclusion of women (the purdah system), to be abhorrent to the laws of Islām.

MUSLIM CONCEPTION OF THE HEREAFTER—PARADISE

Islām accepts the doctrines of accountability for human actions in another existence and belief in a future life. The Kur'ān, like other sacred books, gives vivid word-pictures regarding the joys of Paradise and the sufferings of Hell. There are many Muslims who interpret the ornate descriptions in the Kur'ān in their literal sense; but such exoterics are not peculiar to Islām—they will be found among the followers of all religions. Just as some Christians believe that the Cherubs and Seraphs of the Scriptures are tangible beings, there are Muslims who look upon the *Houris and Ghilmans* (the corresponding Arabic terms in the Kur'ān) in a similar way.

In modern times, no Muslim of even average intelligence and culture interprets the descriptions in the Kur'ān in their literal sense, and would refute most emphatically that any Muslim, no matter how dull and untutored his mind, looks forward to sensual enjoyment in the next world. The similes and descriptions given in the Kur'ān are worded in such a manner as to be easily understood by the people to whom they were addressed. To the parched, toiling and destitute Arab of the desert, constantly engaged in internecine warfare, what could more vividly depict his ideals of happiness, dignity and comfort than a Paradise which is a garden, shady and evergreen, with murmuring streams of pure water, an unending season of fruits, stately mansions luxuriously furnished, and handsome attendants—no necessity for work, only peace and plenty. That these are allegorical descriptions will be clear from verse 35 of chapter xiii of the Kur'ān: 'The likeness, or similitude, of the Heaven which the righteous are promised is a garden beneath which flow rivers; perpetual is the enjoyment thereof, its food is everlasting, and the shade thereof. Such is the reward of the righteous.' The direction to follow the spirit and not the letter of the teachings of the Kur'ān is clear from verse 6 of chapter iii: 'It is He who hath revealed unto thee the Book (the Kur'ān). Some of its verses are decisive, clear to understand—they are the basis of the Book—and others are allegorical. Those in whose hearts is perversity follow the part that is allegorical, seeking to mislead, and seeking to give it (their own) interpretation.'

From the following quotations it will be obvious that the Kur'ān promises a spiritual Paradise:

xiii. 21–4: 'Those who bear calamity with fortitude, seeking the bliss of the countenance of their Lord: ... Gardens of perpetual bliss they shall enter there . . . and angels shall enter unto them from every gate; Peace be unto you for that ye patiently endured calamity! Now how excellent is the final Home!'

lii. 23: 'There they pass from hand to hand a cup wherein is neither taint nor cause of sin.'

xv. 47–8: 'And We shall remove evil and rancour from their hearts, they will be as brethren face to face, resting on couches raised. Toil cometh not to them there, nor will they be expelled from thence.'

lvi. 25–6: 'There hear they no vain talk nor recrimination, only the word "Peace ! Peace ! " '

ix. 72: 'God hath promised to Believers, men and women, hallowed dwellings in Gardens under which rivers flow, to abide therein. But greater by far is the Presence of God—that is the supreme felicity.'

iii. 194: 'Never will I suffer to be lost the work of any of you, be ye male or female. Ye are members one of another, of the same human status. . . . I will blot out their iniquities, and admit them into Gardens with rivers flowing beneath, a reward from God—the nearness of His presence is the best of rewards.'

iii. 197: 'For those who are dutiful to their Lord are Gardens, underneath which rivers flow, therein are they to dwell for ever—a gift of the presence of God, and nearness to God is the best bliss for the righteous.'

xxxii. 17: 'No one comprehends the celestial bliss which awaits him, the glory that will illuminate the darkness of his eyes as a reward for his good deeds.' (See Saying 230.)

lxxxix. 27–30: 'O soul, that art at rest, return to thy Lord joyfully with His grace upon thee. Enter thou the fold of My devotees, Yea, enter thou My Heaven.'

With regard to the translations of the Kur'ān on which most of the misconceptions and allegations against Islām have been based, it must be made clear that no synod of learned men was ever commissioned to produce an authentic translation of the Kur'ān from the original Arabic into English or any other language. The existent translations are the result of the efforts of individual translators from time to time, each of whom has put his own meaning to the words, and given interpretation to the context according to his own ideas. It must also be realised that, apart from the fact that the Kur'ān is written in several dialects (see Saying 257), the Arabic language itself is such that the slightest change of vowel points and accent entirely alters the meaning and significance of a sentence, and it is painful to see the mutilations and misrepresentations, some due to honest mistakes owing to lack of familiarity with the idiomatic expressions of the language, and others due to prejudice and venom against the Muslims and their religion. The standard translation in English, by George Sale, a learned Christian missionary, which finds a place in the Chandos Classics, is based on the Latin version of the Kur'ān by Maracci, the confessor of Pope Innocent XI. The object of this work, which was dedicated to the Holy Roman Emperor Leopold I, was to discredit Islām in the eyes of Europe, and Maracci introduces it by an introductory volume containing what he calls 'a refutation of the Kur'ān.' It is a recognised fact of history that in the Dark Ages of the Crusades, truth was constantly perverted for the sake of political ends. 'To this day, wherever scientific thought has not infused a new soul, wherever true culture has not gained a foothold, the old spirit of exclusiveness and intolerance, the old ecclesiastic hatred of Islām, displays itself in writings, in newspaper attacks, in private conversations, in public speeches.'*

I earnestly trust that the modern spirit of inquiry and broadminded tolerance will prevent the acceptance of these old prejudices, and the publication of this little book in the Wisdom of the East Series will, in the words of the Editor, 'be the ambassador of goodwill and understanding between East and West.'

* *The Spirit of Islam,* page 312.

INDEX TO REFERENCES IN THE CHAPTER ON
ISLĀM

(For quotations from the Kur'ān, see Appendix, pp. 113ff.)

Note No.	Chapter and Verse of the Kur'ān.
1.	iii. 143
2.	ii. 136, and xlii. 13.
3.	xxxv. 24.
4.	xiii. 38.
5.	xlii. 13.
6.	ii. 136.
7.	iv. 171.
8.	ii. 156.
9.	ii. 255, and ii. 163.
10.	v. 39, and xxxix. 53.
11.	ii. 62.
12.	ii. 190.
13.	viii. 61.
14.	ii. 256.
16.	xvii. 31, and xvi, 58–9.
17.	iv. 3, and iv. 129.
18.	xvi. 97, and ii. 228.
19.	iv. 7.
21.	ii. 177.

15.	Marmaduke Pickthall: *The Cultural Side of Islām.*
20.	Judge Pierre Crabites: 'Things Muhammad did for Women', Magazine *Asia*, U.S.A., 1927.
22.	Ablutions: see Appendix, page 115.

The Sayings of Muhammad

بسم الله الرحمن الرحيم *

IN GOD'S NAME, THE MERCIFUL, THE COMPASSIONATE

قال رسول الله صلَعم :

1. Actions will be judged according to intentions.

2. The proof of a Muslim's sincerity is that he payeth no heed to that which is not his business.

3. No man is a true believer unless he desireth for his brother that which he desireth for himself.

4. That which is lawful is clear, and that which is unlawful likewise, but there are certain doubtful things between the two from which it is well to abstain.[1]

---

[1] According to Abu Dā'ūd, only these four sayings of the Prophet are indispensable for the religious guidance of man, and contain the summary of Islāmic law.

Of ABSTINENCE

1. Remember the Lord in retirement from the people and make prayer thy sleep, and hunger thy food.

2. Kill not your hearts with excess of eating and drinking.

3. Illumine your hearts by hunger, and strive to conquer your self by hunger and thirst; continue to knock at the gates of Paradise by hunger.

4. The world is sweet in the heart, and green to the eye; and verily God hath brought you, after those that went before you: then look to your actions, and abstain from the world and its wickedness.

5. The nearest to me are the abstinent, whoever they are, wherever they are.

6. A keeper of the fast, who doth not abandon lying and detraction, God careth not about his leaving off eating and drinking (that is, God doth not accept his fasting).

7. A man once said to Muhammad, "O Messenger of God, permit me to become a eunuch." He said, "That person is not of me who maketh another a eunuch, or becometh so himself; because the manner in which my followers become eunuchs is by fasting and abstinence." The man said, "Permit me to retire from society, and to abandon the delights of the world." He said, "The retirement that becometh my followers is to live in the world and yet to sit in the corner of a mosque in expectation of prayers."

8. A man while fasting must abstain from all bad expressions and must not even resent an injury.

9. Torment not yourselves, lest God should punish you.

10. There is no monasticism in Islām.

11. S'ad b. Abi Wakkās said: "The Apostle forbade 'Uthmān b. Ma'zūn from avoiding marriage: and if he had permitted that to him, verily we (the other Muslims) would have become eunuchs."

12. The friend I most emulate is a Muslim unencumbered; a man of small family, and little money, a performer of prayers and a perfect worshipper of God in private, one who is unknown, and hath enough to supply his wants, and when he dieth, he will leave few women to cry for him, and few legacies.

13. Keep fast and eat also, stay awake at night and sleep also, for verily there is a duty on you to your body, not to labour overmuch, so that ye may not get ill and destroy yourselves; and verily there is a duty on you to your eyes, ye must sometimes sleep and give them rest; and verily there is a duty on you to your wife, and to your visitors and guests that come to see you; ye must talk to them; and nobody hath kept fast who fasted always; the fast of three days in every month is equal to constant fasting: then keep three days' fast in every month.

Of ADULTERY

14. When a man committeth adultery, Imān (Faith) leaveth him; but when he leaveth such evil ways, Imān will return to him.

15. The adultery of the eye is to look with an eye of desire on the wife of another; and the adultery of the tongue is to utter what is forbidden.

16. Ye followers of Muhammad, I swear by God, there is not anything which God so abhors, as adultery.

17. Every eye is an adulterer; and whatever woman perfumeth herself, and goeth to an assembly where men are, wishing to show herself to them, with a look of lasciviousness, is an adulteress. (That is, every eye that looks with desire upon a woman commits adultery.)

Of AGED PERSONS

18. To every young person who honoureth the old, on account of their age, may God appoint those who shall honour him in his years.

19. Verily, to honour an old man is showing respect to God.

Of ALMS-GIVING

20. The best of alms is that which the right hand giveth, and the left hand knoweth not of.

21. The best of almsgiving is that which springeth from the heart, and is uttered by the lips to soften the wounds of the injured.

22. Almsgiving is a duty unto you. Alms should be taken from the rich and returned to the poor.

23. There are seven people whom God will draw under His own shadow, on the day when there will be no other shadow; one of them, a man who hath given alms and concealed it, so that his left hand knew not what his right hand did.

24. Muhammad said, "It is indispensable for every Muslim to give alms." The companions asked, "But if he hath not anything to give?" He said, "If he hath nothing, he must do a work with his hand, by which to obtain something, and benefit himself; and give alms with the remainder." They said, "But if he is not able to do that work, to benefit himself and give alms to others?" The Rasūl (Muhammad) said, "Then he should assist the needy and oppressed." They asked, "What if he is not able to assist the oppressed?" He said, "Then he should exhort people to do good." They asked, "And if he cannot?" He said, "Then let him withhold himself from doing harm to people; for verily that is as alms and charity for him."

25. The people of the Rasūl's (Muhammad's) house killed a goat, and the Rasūl inquired, "What remaineth of it?" 'Ā'ishah said, "Nothing but its shoulder; for we have sent the rest to the poor and neighbours." The Rasūl said, "The whole goat remaineth except its shoulder; that is, that remaineth which ye have given away, and what ye have kept in the house is frail."

26. The angels asked, "O God! Is there anything of Thy creation stronger than rocks?" God said, "Yes; iron is stronger than rocks, for it breaketh them." The angels said, "O Lord! Is there anything of Thy creation stronger than iron?" God said, "Yes; fire is stronger than iron, for it melteth it." And the angels said, "O defender! Is there anything of Thy creation stronger than fire?" God said, "Yes; water overcometh fire: it killeth it and maketh it cold." Then the angels said, "O Lord! Is there anything of Thy creation stronger than water?" God said, "Yes; wind overcometh water: it agitateth it and putteth it in motion." They said, "O our cherisher! Is there anything of Thy creation stronger than wind?" God said, "Yes, the children of Adam, giving alms; that is, those who give with their right hands and conceal it from their left, they overcome all."

27. The most excellent of alms is that of a man of small property, which he has earned by labour, and from which he giveth as much as he is able.

28. Giving alms to the poor hath the reward of one alms; but that given to kindred hath two rewards; one, the reward of alms, the other, the reward of helping relations.

29. A man's first charity should be to his own family, if poor.

Of ANIMALS AND DUTIES OWED THERETO

30. Fear God, in treating dumb animals and ride them when they are fit to be ridden and get off them when they are tired.

31. An adulteress passed by a dog at a well; and the dog was holding out his tongue from thirst, which was near killing him, and the woman drew off her boot, and tied it to the end of her garment, and drew water for the dog, and gave him to drink; and she was forgiven for that act.

32. A woman was punished for a cat, which she tied, till it died from hunger. She gave the cat nothing to eat, nor did she set it at liberty, so that it might find some food.

33. "Are there rewards for our doing good to quadrupeds, and giving them water to drink?" Muhammad said, "Verily there are heavenly rewards for any act of kindness to a live animal."[1]

34. Verily God hath one hundred loving kindnesses; one of which He hath sent down amongst man, quadrupeds

---

[1] In the Kur'ān, animal life stands on the same footing as human life in the sight of God. "There is no beast on earth," says the Kur'ān, "nor bird which flieth with its wings, but the same is a people like unto you (mankind)—and to the Lord shall they return."

and every moving thing upon the face of the earth: by it they are kind to each other, and forgive one another; and by it the animals of the wilds are kind to their young; and God hath reserved ninety-nine loving kindnesses, by which He will be gracious to His creatures on the last day.

35. A man came before the Rasūl with a carpet, and said, "O Rasūl! I passed through a wood, and heard the voices of the young of birds; and I took and put them into my carpet; and their mother came fluttering round my head, and I uncovered the young, and the mother fell down upon them, then I wrapped them up in my carpet; and there are the young which I have." Then the Rasūl said, "Put them down." And when he did so, their mother joined them: and Muhammad said, "Do you wonder at the affection of the mother towards her young? I swear by Him who hath sent me, verily God is more loving to His creatures than the mother to these young birds. Return them to the place from which ye took them, and let their mother be with them."

Of BACKBITING

36. Backbiting vitiates ablution and fasting.

Of BEAUTY

37. Muhammad said: "That person will not enter Paradise who hath one atom of pride in his heart."
And a man present said, "Verily, a man is fond of having good clothes, and good shoes." Muhammad said, "God is

Beauty and delighteth in the beautiful; but pride is holding man in contempt."

Of BEGGING

38. Every man who shall beg, in order to increase his property, God will diminish it.

39. Verily God loveth a Muslim with a family, who is poor, and withholdeth himself from the unlawful and from begging.

40. Whoso openeth unto himself the door of begging, God will open unto him the door of poverty.

41. Verily it is better for any of you to take your rope and bring a bundle of wood upon your back and sell it, in which case God guardeth your honour, than to beg of people, whether they give or not; if they do not give, your reputation suffereth, and you return disappointed; and if they give, it is worse than that, for it layeth you under obligation.

42. Whoever hath food for a day and night, it is prohibited for him to beg.

43. Verily it is not right for the rich to ask, nor for a strong, robust person; but it is allowable for the indigent and the infirm.

44. "May I beg from people, *O Messenger of God*, when necessitous?" Muhammad said, "Do not beg unless absolutely compelled, then only from the virtuous."

Of THE TWO BENEFITS

45. There are two benefits, of which the generality of men are losers, and of which they do not know the value: health and leisure.

Of CHARITY

46. Charity that is concealed appeaseth the wrath of God.

47. Prayers lighten the heart, and charity is a proof of Imān (Faith), and abstinence from sin is perfect splendour; the Kur'ān is a proof of gain to you, if you do good, and it is a detriment to you if you do wrong;[1] and every man who riseth in the morning either doeth that which will be the means of his redemption or his ruin.

48. Charity is a duty unto every Muslim. He who hath not the means thereto, let him do a good act or abstain from an evil one. That is his charity.

49. When you speak, speak the truth; perform when you promise; discharge your trust; commit not fornication; be chaste; have no impure desires; withhold your hands from striking, and from taking that which is unlawful and bad.

[1] Because it promises Happiness to the good and Misery to the wicked.

The best of God's servants are those who, when seen, remind of God; and the worst of God's servants are those who carry tales about, to do mischief and separate friends, and seek for the defects of the good.

50. Whoso hath left debt and children, let them come to me; I am their patron, I will discharge his debt and befriend his children.

51. Every good act is charity.

52. Doing justice between two people is charity; and assisting a man upon his beast, and lifting his baggage, is charity; and pure, comforting words are charity; and answering a questioner with mildness, is charity; and removing that which is an inconvenience to wayfarers, such as thorns and stones, is charity.

53. Every good act is charity; and verily it is a good act to meet your brother with an open countenance, and to pour water from your own water-bag into his vessel.

54. Your smiling in your brother's face, is charity; and your exhorting mankind to virtuous deeds, is charity; and your prohibiting the forbidden, is charity; and your showing men the road, in the land in which they lose it, is charity; and your assisting the blind, is charity.

Of CHASTITY

55. Modesty and chastity are parts of the Faith.

Of CHRISTIANS AND JEWS

56. Muhammad once referred to strife, and said, "It will appear at the time of knowledge leaving the world." Zīād said, "O Messenger of God, how will knowledge go from the world, since we read the Kur'ān, and teach it to our children, and our children to theirs; and so on till the last day?" Then Muhammad said, "O Zīād, I supposed you the most learned man of Medinah. *Do the Jews and Christians who read the Bible and the Evangel act on them?*"

57. Do not exceed bounds in praising me, as the Christians do in praising Jesus, the son of Mary, by calling Him God, and the Son of God; I am only the Lord's servant; then call me the servant of God, and His messenger.

58. When the bier of anyone passeth by thee, whether Jew, Christian or Muslim, rise to thy feet.

Of CLEANLINESS

59. Were it not for fear of troubling my disciples, verily I would order them to clean their teeth before every prayer.[1]

60. God is pure and loveth purity and cleanliness.

---

[1] A Muslim prays five times a day, and each prayer is preceded by the prescribed ablution. (See page 115.)

Of COMPASSION

61. When the child (of Zainab) was brought to Muham-mad, dying; its body trembling and moving; the eyes of the Apostle of God shed many tears. And S'ad said, "O Messenger of God! What is this weeping and shedding of tears?"[1] Muhammad replied, "This is an expression of the tenderness and compassion, which the Lord hath put into the hearts of His servants; the Lord doth not have compassion on and commiserate with His servants, except such as are tender and full of feeling."

62. The Apostle of God wept over S'ad b. 'Ubādah. And he said, "Have not you heard that the Lord doth not punish on account of shedding tears, nor for sobs from the hearts of the afflicted?" He is not of the people of our way who slappeth his cheeks and teareth his collar, and mourneth like the mournings of Ignorance.[2]

63. There is no reward but Paradise for a Muslim who suffereth with patience when the soul of his affectionate friend is taken.

64. Once Muhammad went together with some of his companions to Abū Yūsuf, a blacksmith who was the husband of the nurse of Muhammad's son Ibrahīm. And the Apostle of God took Ibrahīm and kissed him and embraced

[1] The disciples expected the Messenger of God to be above smiles and tears.

[2] The Prophet had forbidden 'the mournings of Ignorance' (the Dark Age of Arabia, or the Age of Idolatry)—loud lamentations, wailings, slapping the cheeks, etc.—but not the silent grief of the heart.

him. On another occasion they went to see Ibrahīm, when he was in his dying moments. Then the eyes of Muhammad were fixed, and flowed with tears; and 'Abd-al-Rahmān, son of 'Auf, said to the Messenger of God, "Do you weep and shed tears, O Apostle of God?" He said, "O son of 'Auf, these tears are compassion, and feeling due to the dead." After that he shed tears again, and said, "Verily my eyes shed tears and my heart is afflicted, and I say nothing but what is pleasing to my Benefactor; for verily, O Ibrahīm, I am melancholy at being separated from thee."

65. Muhammad asked, "Do you think this woman will cast her own child into the fire?" Those present said, "No." Muhammad said, "Verily God is more compassionate on His creatures, than this woman on her own child."

66. When one of the family of Muhammad died, and the women assembled, crying over the corpse, Omar stood up to prevent them from crying, and drive them away: but Muhammad said, "Let them alone, O Omar, because eyes are shedders of tears; and the heart is stricken with calamity and sorrowful; and the time of misfortune is near and fresh; and the crying of the women is without wailing."

Of CONSCIENCE

67. A man asked Muhammad what was the mark whereby he might know the reality of his faith. Muhammad said: "If thou derive pleasure from the good which thou hast performed and thou be grieved for the evil which thou hast

committed, thou art a true believer." The man said: "In what doth a fault really consist?" Muhammad said: "When anything pricketh thy conscience, forsake it."

68. All actions are judged by the motives prompting them.

Of CONTENTMENT

69. Riches are not from abundance of worldly goods, but from a contented mind.

70. When you see a person, who has been given more than you in money and beauty; then look to those who have been given less.

71. Look to those inferior to yourselves, so that you may not hold God's benefits in contempt.

72. God loveth those who are content.

Of CONTROL OF SELF

73. The most excellent Jihād (Holy war) is that for the conquest of self.

74. The exercise of religious duties will not atone for the fault of an abusive tongue.

75. A man cannot be a Muslim till his heart and tongue are so.[1]

76. Whoever hath been given gentleness, hath been given a good portion, in this world and the next.

77. Whoever suppresseth his anger, when he hath in his power to show it, God will give him a great reward.

78. That person is wise and sensible who subdueth his carnal desires and hopeth for rewards from God; and he is an ignorant man who followeth his lustful appetites, and with all this asketh God's forgiveness.

79. May God fill the heart of that person who suppresseth his anger with safety and faith.

80. "Give me advice," said someone. Muhammad said, "Be not angry."

81. Mu'āz said, "At the time of my being dispatched to the judgeship of Yemen, the last advice Muhammad gave me was this, 'O Mu'āz! Be of good temper towards people.'"

82. He is not strong and powerful, who throweth people down; but he is strong who withholdeth himself from anger.

83. No person hath drunk a better draught than that of anger which he hath swallowed for God's sake.

---

[1] The Islām of heart is its purity; and the Islām of the tongue withholding it from fruitless words.

Of COURTESY

84. Humility and courtesy are acts of piety.

85. Verily, a man teaching his child manners is better for him than giving one bushel of grain in alms.

86. It is not right for a guest to stay so long as to incommode his host.

87. No father hath given his child anything better the good manners.

88. "O Apostle of God! Inform me, if I stop with a man, and he doth not entertain me, and he afterwards stoppeth at my house, am I to entertain him or act with him as he did with me?" Muhammad said, "Entertain him."

89. Respect people according to their eminence.

90. Being confined for room, the Apostle of God sat down upon his legs drawn up under his thighs. A desert Arab who was present said, "What is this way of sitting?" Muhammad said, "Verily God hath made me a humble servant, and not a proud king."

91. Abuse nobody, and if a man abuse thee, and lay open a vice which he knoweth in thee; then do not disclose one which thou knowest in him.

92. When victuals are placed before you no man must stand up till it be taken away; nor must one man leave off

eating before the rest; and if he doeth, he must make an apology.[1]

93. It is of my ways that a man shall come out with his guest to the door of his house.

94. Meekness and modesty are two branches of Imān (Faith); and vain talking and embellishing are two branches of hypocrisy.

95. When three persons are together, two of them must not whisper to each other without letting the third hear, until others are present, because it would hurt him.

Of CRIMES

96. The greatest crimes are to associate another with God, to vex your father and mother, to murder your own species, to commit suicide, and to swear to a lie.

Of CULTIVATION OF LAND

97. There is no Muslim who planteth a tree, or soweth a field, and man, birds or beasts eat from them, but it is charity for him.

98. Whoever bringeth the dead land to life; that is, cultivateth waste land, for him is reward therein.

---

[1] Imam Ja'far Sādik said: "The Apostle used, when he ate in company, to eat to the last, and did not leave off before others."

Of THE DEAD

99. And behold! A bier passed by Muhammad, and he stood up; and it was said to him, " This is the bier of a Jew." He said, "Was it not the holder of a soul, from which we should take example and fear?"

100. Muhammad passed by some graves in Medinah, and turned his face toward them, and said, "Peace to you, O people of the graves! May God forgive us and you: You have passed on before us, and we are following you!"

101. Do not speak ill of the dead.

102. When the bier of anyone passeth by thee, whether Jew, Christian, or Muslim, rise to thy feet.

Of DEATH

103. Wish not for death, any one of you; neither the doer of good works, for peradventure he may increase them by an increase of life; nor the offender, for perhaps he may obtain the forgiveness of God by repentance. Wish not, nor supplicate for death before its time cometh; for verily when ye die, hope is out and the ambition for reward: and verily, the increase of a Mu'min's (Muslim's) life increaseth his good works.

104. Remember often the destroyer and cutter-off of delights, which is death.

105. Not one of you must wish for death, from any worldly affliction; but if there certainly is anyone wishing for death, he must say, "O Lord, keep me alive so long as life may be good for me, and cause me to die when it is better for me so to do."

106. The Faithful do not die; perhaps they become translated from this perishable world to the world of eternal existences.

107. Death is a blessing to a Muslim. Remember and speak well of your dead, and refrain from speaking ill of them.

108. There are two things disliked by the sons of Adam, one of them death: whereas it is better for Muslims than sinning; the second is scarcity of money: whereas its account will be small in futurity.

109. The grave is the first stage of the journey into eternity.

110. Death is a bridge that uniteth friend with friend.

111. Sleep is the brother of death.

112. Muhammad said, three days before his death, "Not one of you must die but with resignation to the will of God, and with hope for His beneficence and pardon."

Of DEBT

113. Whoso desireth that God should redeem him from the sorrows and travail of the last day, must delay in calling on poor debtors, or forgive the debt in part or whole.

114. A martyr shall be pardoned every fault but debt.

115. Whoso hath a thing wherewith to discharge a debt, and refuseth to do it, it is right to dishonour and punish him.

Of DELIBERATION

116. Deliberation in undertakings is pleasing to God.

117. A good disposition, and deliberation in affairs, and a medium in all things, are one part of twenty-four parts of the qualities of the prophets.

Of THE DISPOSITION TO GOOD

118. He is of the most perfect Muslims, whose disposition is most liked by his own family.

119. Verily the most beloved of you by me, and nearest to me in the next world, are those of good dispositions; and verily the greatest enemies to me and the farthest from me, are the ill-tempered.

120. Verily, the most beloved of you by me are those of the best dispositions.

121. I have been sent to explain fully good dispositions.

122. O Lord! As thou hast made my body good, so make good my disposition.

123. Two qualities are not combined in any Muslim, avarice and bad disposition.

Of DISPUTATION

124. Mankind will not go astray after having found the right road, unless from disputation.

Of DIVORCE

125. Every woman who asketh to be divorced from her husband without cause, the fragrance of the Garden is forbidden her.

126. The thing which is lawful, but disliked by God, is divorce.

Of THE DUTY OF BELIEVERS

127. I have left two things among you, and you will not stray as long as you hold them fast; one is the Book of God, the other the Laws of His Messenger.

128. God hath made a straight road, with two walls, one on each side of it, in which are open doors, with curtains drawn across. At the top of the road is an Admonisher, who saith, "Go straight on the road, and not crooked"; and above this Admonisher is another who saith to any one who would pass through these doorways, "Pass not through those doors, or verily ye will fall." Now, the road is Islām; and the open doors, are those things which God hath forbidden; and the curtains before the doors the bounds set by God; the Admonisher is the Kur'ān, and the upper Admonisher *God, in the heart of every Mu'min* (Muslim).

129. Verily ye are ordered the divine commandments, then forsake them not; ye are forbidden the unlawful, then do not fall therein; there are fixed boundaries, then pass not beyond them; and there is silence on some things without their being forgotten, then do not debate about them.

130. Happy is the Mu'min (Muslim), for, if good befalleth him, he praiseth and thanketh God; and, if misfortune, praiseth God and beareth it patiently; therefore a Mu'min is rewarded for every good he doth, even for his raising a morsel of food to the mouth of his wife.

131. Whoever hath eaten of pure food and practised my laws, and mankind hath lived in security from him, will enter into the Abode of Bliss.

132. Muhammad once said to Anas, "Son, if you are able, keep your heart from morning till night and from night till morning, free from malice towards anyone"; then he said, "Oh! My son, this is one of my laws, and he who loveth my laws verily loveth me."

133. I admonish you to fear God, and yield obedience to my successor, although he may be a black slave, for this reason, that those amongst you who may live after me will see great schisms. Therefore hold fast to my ways and those of my successors, who may lead you in the straight path, having found it themselves; and ardently seize my laws and be firm thereto.

134. There was not any Messenger sent before me by God to mankind but found friends and companions, who embraced his maxims and became his disciples; after which were born those who gave out precepts which they did not practise, and did what they were not ordered to do: therefore those who oppose them with the hand, with the tongue, and with the heart are Mu'mins, and there is not anything in Imān besides this, even as much as a grain of mustard seed.

135. Do not associate any one thing with God, although they kill or burn you; nor affront intentionally your parents, although they should order you to quit your wife, your children, and your property. Do not drink wine; for it is the root of all evil; abstain from vice; and when a pestilence shall pervade mankind, and you shall be amongst them, remain with them; and cherish your children.

136. There are three roots to Imān (Faith): not to trouble him who shall say 'there is no deity but God'; not to think him an unbeliever on account of one fault; and not to discard him for one crime.[1]

---

[1] Provided a person believes in the cardinal doctrines of Islām (page 20) no one can say he is not a Muslim. God will forgive his sins. (See Note No. 10, page 114.)

137. He is not a good Mu'min who committeth adultery or getteth drunk, who stealeth, or plundereth, or who embezzleth; beware, beware.

138. When asked to mention one of the most excellent parts of Imān (Faith) Muhammad said, "To love him who loveth God, and hate him who hateth God, and to keep your tongue employed in repeating the name of God." What else? He said, "To do unto all men as you would wish to have done unto you, and to reject for others what you would reject for yourself."

139. He who progresseth daily is yet far off from the Ideal.

140. When you speak, speak the truth; perform when you promise; discharge your trust; commit not fornication; be chaste; have no impure desires; withhold your hands from striking, and from taking that which is unlawful or evil. The best of God's servants are those who, when seen, remind of God; and the worst of God's servants are those who carry tales about, to do mischief and separate friends, and seek for the defects of the good.

141. He who believeth in one God and the Hereafter (i.e., a Muslim), let him speak what is good or remain silent.

142. He who believeth in one God and the life beyond (i.e., a Muslim), let him not injure his neighbours.

143. Speak to men according to their mental capacities, for if you speak all things to all men, some cannot understand you, and so fall into errors.

144. It is not a sixth or a tenth of a man's devotion which is acceptable to God, but only such portions thereof as he offereth with understanding and true devotional spirit.

145. Verily your deeds will be brought back to you, as if you yourself were the creator of your own punishment.

146. Adore God as thou wouldst if thou sawest Him; for, if thou seest Him not, He seeth thee.

147. Feed the hungry and visit the sick, and free the captive, if he be unjustly confined. Assist any person oppressed, whether Muslim or non-Muslim.

148. "The duties of Muslims to each other are six." It was asked, "What are they, O Messenger of God?" He said, "When you meet a Muslim, greet him, and when he inviteth you to dinner, accept; and when he asketh you for advice, give it him; and when he sneezeth and saith, 'Praise be to God', do you say, 'May God have mercy upon thee'; and when he is sick, visit him; and when he dieth, follow his bier."

149. This life is but a tillage for the next, do good that you may reap there; for striving is the ordinance of God and whatever God hath ordained can only be attained by striving.

150. Commandments are of three kinds; one commands an action, the reward of which is clear, then do it; another forbids an action which leads astray, abstain from it; and in another arise contradictions, resign that to God.

151. The world is forbidden to those of the life to come; the life to come is forbidden to those of this world.

152. Do a good deed after every bad deed that it may blot out the latter.

153. A true Mu'min (Muslim) is thankful to God in prosperity, and resigned to His will in adversity.

154. That which is lawful is clear, and that which is unlawful likewise: but there are certain doubtful things between the two from which it is well to abstain.

155. Be ye imbued with divine qualities.

156. He is true who protecteth his brethren both present and absent.

157. All Muslims are as one body. If a man complaineth of a pain in his head, his whole body complaineth; and if his eye complaineth, his whole body complaineth.

158. All Muslims are like the component parts of a foundation, each strengthening the others; in such a way must they support each other.

159. Assist your brother Muslim, whether he be an oppressor or an oppressed. "But how shall we do it when he is an oppressor?" inquired a companion. Muhammad replied, "Assisting an oppressor consists in forbidding and withholding him from oppression."

160. Muslims are brothers in religion and they must not oppress one another, nor abandon assisting each other, nor hold one another in contempt. The seat of righteousness is the heart; therefore that heart which is righteous, does not hold a Muslim in contempt; and all the things of one Muslim are unlawful to another; his blood, property and reputation.

161. The creation is as God's family; for its sustenance is from Him: therefore the most beloved unto God is the person who doeth good to God's family.

162. The proof of a Muslim's sincerity is that he payeth no heed to that which is not his business.

163. The Faithful are those who perform their trust and fail not in their word, and keep their pledge.

164. No man is a true believer unless he desireth for his brother that which he desireth for himself.

165. Verily when a Muslim is taken ill, after which God restoreth him to health, his illness hath covered his former faults, and it is an admonition to him of what cometh in future times; and verily, when a hypocrite is taken ill, and afterwards restored to health, he is like a camel which hath been tied up, and afterwards set free; for the camel did not know for want of discrimination, why they tied him up and why they let him loose; such is the hypocrite: on the contrary, a Mu'min knoweth, that his indisposition was to atone for his faults.

166. Misfortune is always with the Muslim and his wife, either in their persons or their property or children; either death or sickness; until they die, when there is no fault upon them.

167. Abusing a Muslim is disobedience to God; and it is infidelity to fight with one.

168. Every man who calls a Muslim infidel will have the epithet returned to him.

169. It is unworthy of a Mu'min to injure people's reputations; and it is unworthy to curse anyone; and it is unworthy to abuse anyone; and it is unworthy of a Mu'min to talk vainly.

170. It is better to sit alone than in company with the bad; and it is better to sit with the good than alone. And it is better to speak words to a seeker of knowledge than to remain silent; and silence is better than bad words.

171. Fear not the obloquy of the detractor in showing God's religion.

172. Refrain from seeing and speaking of the vices of mankind, which you know are in yourself.

173. Guard yourselves from six things, and I am your security for Paradise. When you speak, speak the truth; perform when you promise; discharge your trust; be chaste in thought and action; and withhold your hand from striking, from taking that which is unlawful, and bad.

174. That person is not of us who inviteth others to aid him in oppression; and he is not of us who fighteth for his tribe in injustice; and he is not of us who dieth in assisting his tribe in tyranny.

175. He is not of us who is not affectionate to his little ones, and doth not respect the feelings of the aged: and he is not of us who doth not order that which is good and prohibit that which is evil.

176. Ye will not enter Paradise until ye have faith, and ye will not complete your faith until ye love one another.

177. No man hath believed perfectly, until he wish for his brother that which he wisheth for himself.

178. Verily, each of you is a mirror to his brother: then if he seeth a vice in his brother he must tell him to get rid of it.

179. That person is not a perfect Muslim who eateth his fill, and leaveth his neighbours hungry.

180. O ye who have embraced Islām by the tongue, and to whose hearts it hath not reached, distress not Muslims, nor speak ill of them, nor seek for their defects.

181. Do not say, that if people do good to us, we will do good to them; and if people oppress us, we will oppress them; but determine, that if people do you good, you will do good to them; and if they oppress you, you will not oppress them.

182. "Teach me a work, such that when I perform it God and men will love me." Muhammad said: "Desire not the world, and God will love you; and desire not what men have, and they will love you."

183. In prayers, all thoughts must be laid aside, but those of God; in conversation, no word is to be uttered which may afterwards be repented of; do not covet from others, or have any hopes from them.

184. "There is a polish for everything that taketh away rust; and the polish for the heart is the remembrance of God." The companions said, "Is not repelling the infidels also like this?" Muhammad said, "No, although one fights until one's sword be broken!"

185. My Lord hath commanded me nine things: (1) To reverence Him, externally and internally; (2) to speak the truth, and with propriety, in prosperity and adversity; (3) moderation in affluence and poverty; (4) to benefit my relations and kindred, who do not benefit me; (5) to give alms to him who refuseth me; (6) to forgive him who injureth me; (7) that my silence should be in attaining a knowledge of God; (8) that when I speak, I should mention Him; (9) that when I look on God's creatures, it should be as an example for them: and God hath ordered me to direct in that which is lawful.

186. A Muslim who mixeth with people and beareth inconveniences, is better than one who doth not mix with them and beareth no inconveniences.

Of ELOQUENCE

187. Some eloquence is like magic.

Of ENVY

188. If envy were proper, two persons would be the most proper objects of it; one, a man to whom God hath given riches, and appointed to bestow in charity; the other, to whom God hath granted the knowledge of religion, and who acteth thereon himself, instructing others.

189. Keep yourselves far from envy; because it eateth up and taketh away good actions, like as fire eateth up and burneth wood.

Of EXPERIENCE

190. He is not a perfect man of fortitude, who hath not fallen into misfortunes; and there is no physician but the experienced.

Of FORGIVENESS

191. Thus saith the Lord, "Verily those who are patient in adversity and forgive wrongs, are the doers of excellence."

192. Once Muhammad was asked, "O Apostle of God ! How many times are we to forgive our servants' faults?"

He was silent. Again the questioner asked, and Muhammad gave no answer. But when the man asked a third time, he said, "Forgive your servants seventy times a day."

193. There is no man who is wounded and pardoneth the giver of the wound but God will exalt his dignity and diminish his faults.

194. That person is nearest to God, who pardoneth, when he hath in his power him who would have injured him.

195. Do not say, that if people do good to us, we will do good to them; and if people oppress us, we will oppress them; but determine, that if people do you good, you will do good to them; and if they oppress you, you will not oppress them.

Of GENTLENESS

196. Verily, God is mild, and is fond of mildness, and he giveth to the mild what he doth not to the harsh.

197. Whoever hath been given gentleness hath been given a good portion, in this world and the next.

198. God is gentle and loveth gentleness.

199. Verily you[1] have two qualities which God and His messenger love—fortitude and gentleness.

[1] Ashbah, chief of the embassy from 'Abd-al-kais.

Of GOD

200. Whoever loveth to meet God, God loveth to meet him.

201. God saith, "I fulfill the faith of whoso putteth his faith in Me; and I am with him, and near him, when he remembereth Me."

202. God saith, "Whoso doth one good act, for him are ten rewards; and I also give more to whomever I will; and whoso doth an ill, its punishment is equal to it, or I forgive him; and whoso seeketh to approach Me one span, I seek to approach one cubit; and whoso seeketh to approach Me one cubit, I seek to approach him two fathoms; and whoso walketh towards Me, I run towards him; and whoso cometh before Me with the earth full of sins, and believeth solely in Me, him I come before with a front of forgiveness as big as the earth."

203. God saith, "The person I hold as a beloved, I am his hearing by which he heareth, and I am his sight by which he seeth, and I am his hands by which he holdeth, and I am his feet by which he walketh."

204. God saith, "O Man! Only follow thou My laws, and thou shalt become like unto Me, and then say, 'Be' and behold, It is."[1]

---

[1] I.e., if a person is in tune with the universe and in complete harmony with the laws of nature, then his will is in accord with the Divine will and whatever such a person willeth cometh to pass.

205. God is One, and liketh unity.

206. We were with Muhammad on a journey, and some men stood up repeating aloud, "God is most great," and the Rasūl said, "O men! Be easy on yourselves, and do not distress yourselves by raising your voices; verily you do not call to one deaf or absent, but verily to one who heareth and seeth; and He is with you; and He to whom you pray is nearer to you than the neck of your camel."[1]

207. God saith, "I was a hidden treasure. I would fain be known. So I created Man."

208. Do you love your Creator? Love your fellow-beings first.

Of GOD'S FORGIVENESS

209. Muhammad said, "I would not have the whole wealth of the world in the place of this revelation." "Say: (O Muhammad!) O My servants who have oppressed your own souls by sinning, despair not of the mercy of God."[2] A man said, "What of him who hath associated others with God?" Muhammad remained silent for a while and then said, "Know that him also God forgiveth; but on repentance."

---

[1] Cf. 'We are nearer him (man) than his own vital vein.'— Kur'ān, 1. 15.

[2] xxix, 53 (page 114, Appendix Note 10). 'Verily all sins doth God forgive; aye, Loving, Merciful, is He! And return ye to your Lord, and to Him resign yourselves, ere it is too late.'—Kur'ān, xxxix, 54.

210. God saith, "Verily My compassion overcometh My wrath."

Of GOD'S KINDNESS

211. If the unbeliever knew of the extent of the Lord's mercy, even he would not despair of Paradise.

212. God's kindness towards His creatures is more than a mother's towards her babe.

213. If you put your whole trust in God, as you ought, He most certainly will give you sustenance, as He doth the birds; they come out hungry in the morning, but return full to their nests.

214. Trust in God, but tie it (your camel).

215. God is not merciful to him who is not so to mankind.

216. "Do none enter the Garden of Bliss save by God's mercy?" Muhammad said, "No. None enter save through God's favour." "You also, O Messenger of God! Will you not enter Paradise save by God's compassion?" Muhammad put his hand on his head and said thrice, "I also shall not enter unless God cover me with His mercy."

Of GOOD WORKS

217. That person who relieveth a Mu'min (Muslim) from distress in this world, God will in the like manner relieve

him in the next; and he who shall do good to the indigent, God will do good to him in this world and the next.

218. Be persistent in good actions.

Of THE HEART

219. Beware! Verily there is a piece of flesh in the body of man, which, when good, the whole body is good; and, when bad, the whole body is bad, and that is the heart.

220. Muhammad said, "O Wābīṣah! Are you come to ask what is goodness and what is badness?" Wābīṣah said, "Yes, I am come for that." Then he joined his fingers and struck them upon Wābīṣah's breast, that is, made a sign towards his heart, and said, "Ask the question from thine own heart." This he repeated three times and said, "Goodness is a thing from which thy heart findeth firmness and rest; and badness is a thing which throweth thee into doubt, although men may acquit thee."

Of HEAVEN AND HELL

221. Hell is veiled in delights, and Heaven in hardships and miseries.

222. Heaven lieth at the feet of mothers.

223. He will not enter hell, who hath faith equal to mustard seed in his heart; and he will not enter Paradise, who hath a single grain of pride, equal to a mustard seed in his heart.

224. Paradise is nearer you than the thongs of your sandals; and the Fire likewise.

225. Deal gently with the people, and be not harsh; cheer them and condemn them not. Ye will meet with many 'people of the book' who will question thee, what is the key to heaven? Reply to them (the key to heaven is) to testify to the truth of God, and to do good work.

226. People asked Muhammad if to say "There is no deity but God" was not the key to Paradise. He said, "Yes: but it is a key which hath wards; and if ye come with a key of that description, Paradise will be opened to you, otherwise it will not."

227. Paradise is not for him who reproacheth others with any favour he doeth to them.

228. The people entitled to the Abode of Bliss are three; the first, a just king, a doer of good to his people endowed with virtue; the second, an affectionate man, of a tender heart to relations and others; the third, a virtuous man.

229. Verily a man used to come before the Rasūl (Muhammad), bringing his son with him; and the Rasūl said to him, "Dost thou love this boy?" And the man said, "O Rasūl of God! May God love thee as I love this son!" Then the Rasūl did not see the boy with his father for some time; and he said, "What has become of that man's son?" They said, "O Rasūl! He is dead." And the Rasūl said to the man, "Dost thou not like this, that thou wilt find no door of Paradise but thy son will be there awaiting thee, in order to

conduct thee into Paradise?" And another man said, "O Rasūl! Is this joyful news particularly for this man, or for the whole of us?" Lord Muhammad said, "For all of you."

230. What is Paradise? Muhammad replied, "It is what the eye hath not seen, nor the ear heard, nor ever flashed across the mind of man."

Of HOSPITALITY

231. He who believeth in one God and in a future life (i.e., a Muslim), let him honour his guest.

232. Whoever believeth in God and the Hereafter (i.e., a Muslim) must respect his guest: and whoever believeth in God and the Hereafter must not incommode his neighbours; and a Mu'min must speak only good words, otherwise remain silent.

233. It is not right for a guest to stay so long as to incommode his host.

Of HUMILITY

234. Humility and courtesy are acts of piety.

235. Verily God instructs me to be humble and lowly and not proud; and that no one should oppress another.

236. A tribe must desist from boasting of their forefathers; if they will not leave off boasting, verily they will be more

abominable near God, than a black beetle which rolleth forward filth by its nose; and verily God has removed from you pride and arrogance. There is no man but either a righteous Mu'min or a sinner; mankind are all the sons of Adam, and he was from earth.

237. Whoever is humble to men for God's sake, may God exalt his eminence.

Of ISLĀM

238. "Inform me in the matter of Islām," said Sufyān, "so that I may have no occasion to ask others about it." Muhammad said, "Say, O Sufyān, 'I believe in God'; after which obey the commandments, and abandon the things forbidden."

239. Islām commenced in a forlorn state, and it will quickly return to what it was in the beginning; then be joyful, ye who are firm.

240. My religion is like clouds dropping much rain; some of them, falling on pure, favourable soil, cause fresh grass to grow; some of them fall in hollows from which mankind are benefited, some fall on high lands from which benefit is not derived; then the two first are like the persons acquainted with the religion of God and instructing others; and the last like the person not regarding it nor accepting the right path.

241. The greatest enemies of God are those who are entered into Islām, and do acts of infidelity, and who, without cause, shed the blood of man.

242. When asked, "What is Islām?" Muhammad said, "Abstinence and Obedience to God." Asked "What is one of the most excellent virtues of Imān (Faith)?" he said, "An amiable disposition." "Which is the most excellent Hijrah (Renunciation)?"[1] He said, "Abandoning that of which God disapproveth."

243. "What is Islām?" someone asked. Muhammad said, "Purity of speech and charity."

244. Every child is born with a disposition towards the natural religion (Islām—submission to the Divine Will). It is the parents who make it a Jew, a Christian or a Magian.[2]

245. Do you know what sappeth the foundations of Islām, and ruineth it? The errors of the learned destroy it, and the disputations of the hypocrite, and the orders of kings who have lost the road.

246. Men differ like mines of gold and silver: the good in ignorance are the good in Islām, once they have obtained the knowledge of religion.

---

[1] See page 107.
[2] Hence, according to Islām the souls of 'unbaptised' babes are not lost.

Of KINDNESS

247. To gladden the heart of the weary, to remove the suffering of the afflicted, hath its own reward. In the day of trouble, the memory of the action cometh like a rush of the torrent, and taketh our burden away.

248. He who helpeth his fellow creature in the hour of need, and he who helpeth the oppressed, him will God help in the Day of Travail.

249. What actions are most excellent? To gladden the heart of a human being, to feed the hungry, to help the afflicted, to lighten the sorrow of the sorrowful, and to remove the wrongs of the injured.

250. Who is the most favoured of God? He from whom the greatest good cometh to His creatures.

251. All God's creatures are His family; and he is the most beloved of God who doeth most good to God's creatures.

252. Whoever is kind to His creatures, God is kind to him; therefore be kind to man on earth, whether good or bad; and being kind to the bad, is to withhold him from badness, thus in Heaven you will be treated kindly.

253. He who is not kind to God's creatures, and to his own children, God will not be kind to him.

254. Kindness is a mark of faith: and whoever hath no kindness hath not faith.

Of THE KUR'ĀN

255. The Kur'ān consisteth of five heads, things lawful, things unlawful, clear and positive precepts, mysteries, and examples. Then consider that lawful which is there declared to be so, and that which is forbidden as unlawful; obey the precepts, believe in the mysteries, and take warning from the examples.

256. Doth any one of you suppose that God hath not forbidden anything except in the Kur'ān? Beware, for verily I swear by God that I have ordered, and prohibited things in manner like the Kur'ān: and God hath not made it lawful for you to enter the houses of the People of the Book (that is Jews, Christians, etc.) without their permission, or that you beat their women, or eat their fruits.

257. The Kur'ān was sent down in seven dialects; and in every one of its sentences, there is an external and internal meaning.

258. The other messengers of God had their miracles; mine is the Kur'ān and will remain for ever.

259. "By what rule", said Muhammad, "would you be guided, O Mu'āz, in your administration of Yemen?" "By the law of the Kur'ān." "But if you find no direction in the Kur'ān?" "Then I will act according to the example of the Messenger of God." "But if that faileth?" "Then I will exercise my own reason and judgment."

Of LABOUR

260. Pray to God morning and evening, and employ the day in your avocations.

261. He who neither worketh for himself, nor for others, will not receive the reward of God.

262. Whoso is able and fit and doth not work for himself, or for others, God is not gracious to him.

263. Those who earn an honest living are the beloved of God.

264. God is gracious to him that earneth his living by his own labour, and not by begging.

265. Whoever desireth the world and its riches, in a law-ful manner, in order to withhold himself from begging, and for a livelihood for his family, and for being kind to his neighbour, will come to God with his face bright as the full moon on the fourteenth night of the lunar month.

266. Give the labourer his wage before his perspiration be dry.

Of LEARNING

267. He dieth not who giveth life to learning.

268. Whoso honoureth the learned, honoureth me.

269. The Messenger of God was asked, "What is the greatest vice of man?" He said, "You must not ask me about vice, but ask about virtue;" and he repeated this three times, after which he said, "Know ye! The worst of men is a bad learned man, and a good learned man is the best."

270. Verily God doth not take away knowledge from the hands of His servants; but taketh it by taking away the learned; so that when no learned men remain, the ignorant will be placed at the head of affairs. Causes will be submitted to their decision, they will pass sentence without knowledge, will err themselves, and lead others into error.

271. An hour's contemplation is better than a year's adoration.

272. Philosophy is the stray camel of the Faithful, take hold of it wherever ye come across it.

273. Go in quest of knowledge even unto China.[1]

274. Seek knowledge from the cradle to the grave.

275. The knowledge from which no benefit is derived is like a treasure from which no charity is bestowed in the way of the Lord.

276. Do you know what sappeth the foundation of Islām, and ruineth it? The errors of the learned destroy it, and the

---

[1] I.e., even unto the 'edge of the earth'.

disputations of the hypocrite, and the orders of kings who have lost the road.

277. To spend more time in learning is better than spending more time in praying; the support of religion is abstinence. It is better to teach knowledge one hour in the night than to pray the whole night.

278. Whoever seeketh knowledge and findeth it, will get two rewards; one of them the reward for desiring it, and the other for attaining it; therefore, even if he do not attain it, for him is one reward.

279. That person who shall die while he is studying, in order to revive the knowledge of religion, will be only one degree inferior to the prophets.

280. One learned man is harder on the devil than a thousand ignorant worshippers. The pursuit of knowledge is a divine commandment for every Muslim; and to waste knowledge on those who are unworthy of it is like putting pearls, jewels, and gold on the necks of swine.

281. That person who shall pursue the path of knowledge, God will direct him to the path of Paradise; and verily the superiority of a learned man over an ignorant worshipper is like that of the full moon over all the stars.

282. He who knoweth his own self, knoweth God.

283. Verily the best of God's servants are just and learned kings; and verily the worst are bad and ignorant kings.

284. To listen to the words of the learned, and to instill into others the lessons of science, is better than religious exercises.

285. The ink of the scholar is more holy than the blood of the martyr.

286. He who leaveth home in search of knowledge, walketh in the path of God.

287. One hour's meditation on the work of the Creator is better than seventy years of prayer.

288. God hath treasuries beneath the Throne, the keys whereof are the tongues of poets.

289. The acquisition of knowledge is a duty incumbent on every Muslim, male and female.

290. Acquire knowledge. It enableth its possessor to distinguish right from wrong; it lighteth the way to Heaven; it is our friend in the desert, our society in solitude, our companion when friendless; it guideth us to happiness; it sustaineth us in misery; it is an ornament amongst friends, and an armour against enemies.[1]

291. With knowledge man riseth to the heights of goodness and to a noble position, associateth with sovereigns in this world, and attaineth to the perfection of happiness in the next.

---

[1] The present-day Muslims should bear in mind this remarkable utterance of the 'Illiterate Prophet'.

292. Learn to know thyself.

293. The calamity of knowledge is forgetfulness; and to waste knowledge is to speak of it to the unworthy.

294. Who are the learned? They who practise what they know.

Of MAN'S GROWTH

295. The son of Man groweth and with him grow two things—the love of wealth and love of long life.

296. "Who is the best man?" Muhammad replied, "He is the best man whose life is long and whose actions are good." "Then who is the worst man?" "He whose life is long and whose actions are bad."

Of MARRIAGE

297. Marriage is incumbent on all who possess the ability.

298. A woman may be married by four qualifications: one on account of her money; another, on account of the nobility of her pedigree (Shijra); another, on account of her beauty; the fourth, on account of her virtue. Therefore, look out for a woman that hath virtue: but if you do it from any other consideration, your hands be rubbed in dirt.

Of MEANNESS

299. Shall I tell you the very worst amongst you? Those who eat alone, and whip the slaves, and give to nobody.

Of MISHAPS

300. Whatever mishap may befall you, it is on account of something which you have done.

301. No misfortune or vexation befalleth a servant of God, small or great, but on account of his faults committed: and most of these God forgiveth.

Of MODESTY

302. True modesty is the source of all virtue.

303. Modesty and chastity are parts of the Faith.

304. Meekness and modesty are two branches of Imān; and vain talking and embellishing are two branches of hypocrisy.

305. All kinds of modesty are best.

Of MONOPOLIES

306. Monopoly is unlawful in Islām.

307. The holder of a monopoly is a sinner and offender.

308. The bringers of grain to the city to sell at a cheap rate gain immense advantage by it, and whoso keepeth back grain in order to sell at a high rate is cursed.

Of MOTHERS

309. Heaven lieth at the feet of mothers.

310. "O Messenger of God! Verily I have done a great crime; is there any act by which I may repent?" He said, "Have you a mother?" " No," said the questioner. "Have you an aunt?" asked Muhammad. He said, "Yes, I have." Muhammad said, "Go, do good to her, and your crime will be pardoned."

311. I and a woman whose colour and cheeks shall have become black from toiling in the sun shall be near to one another in the next world as my two fingers; and that is a handsome widow, whose colour and cheeks shall have become black in bringing up her family.

Of MUHAMMAD THE PROPHET

312. I am no more than man; when I order you anything respecting religion, receive it, and when I order you anything about the affairs of the world, then am I nothing more than man.

313. Convey to other persons none of my words, except those ye know of a surety.

314. My sayings do not abrogate the word of God, but the word of God can abrogate my sayings.

315. 'Ā'ishah said, "A party of Jews asked permission to go to Muhammad, and said, 'Death upon you.'[1] And I answered their insult by saying, 'Rather upon you be death and curse.' Then Muhammad said, 'Be mild, O 'Ā'ishah! and make a point of being kind, and withhold thyself from speaking harshly.' I said, 'Did you not hear what they said?' He said, 'Verily, I do always say, "Be the same to you." ' "

316. Verily, my heart is veiled with melancholy and sadness for my followers; and verily I ask pardon of God one hundred times daily.

317. Zaid, Muhammad's servant, said, "I served Lord Muhammad ten years, and he never said 'Uff'[2] to me; and never said, 'Why did you do so?' and never said, 'Why did you not do so?' "

Of MUHAMMAD THE PROPHET'S KINDNESS

318. Once Muhammad was distributing meat in Ji'rānah; and behold a woman came close to him, and he spread his garment for her to sit upon. When people saw such respect shown to this woman, they asked who she was; and those present said, "This is his nurse."

---

[1] Whilst saluting the Muslims the Jews used to 'twist their tongues' and wish them 'death' (السام) (assamo) instead of 'peace' (السلام) (assalamo), words which have a similarity of sound in Arabic.

[2] An exclamation expressive of displeasure.

319. When anyone was sick Muhammad used to rub his hands upon the sick person's body, saying, "O Lord of mankind! Take away this pain, and give health; for Thou art the giver of health: there is no health but Thine, that health which leaveth no sickness."

Of MUHAMMAD THE PROPHET'S MISSION

320. Kais b. S'al said: "I came to Ḥīrah, and saw the inhabitants worshipping their chief; and I said, 'Verily the Apostle of God is worthy of being worshipped.' Then I came to the Apostle and said, 'I saw the people of Ḥīrah worshipping the chief of their tribe, and you are most worthy of being worshipped.' Then Muhammad said to me, 'Tell me, if you should pass by my grave, would you worship it?' I said, 'No.' And he said, 'Worship not me.' "

321. The Apostle was in the midst of a crowd of his companions, and a camel came and prostrated itself before him. They said, "O Apostle of God! Beasts and trees worship thee; then it is meet for us to worship thee." Muhammad said, "Worship God, and you may honour your brother, that is, me."

322. When the ambassadors of Bani 'Āmir went to Muhammad, they said, "You are our master." He said, "God is your master." Then they said, "You are most excellent of the highest degree." And when he heard this, he said, "Say so, or less, and do not exceed reasonable bounds in praise."

323. Muhammad slept upon a mat, and got up very marked on the body by it: and someone said, "O Messenger of God! If thou hadst ordered me, I would have spread a soft bed for thee." Lord Muhammad said, "What business have I with the world? I am like a man on horseback, who standeth under the shade of a tree, then leaveth it."

324. To the light I have attained and in the light I live.[1]

325. It was said to the Rasūl, "O Messenger of God! Curse the infidels." Muhammad said, "I am not sent for this; nor was I sent but as a mercy to mankind."

Of MUHAMMAD THE PROPHET'S PRAYERS

326. Muhammad used to say, after making the profession of faith, "O Lord, I supplicate Thee for firmness in faith, and inclination towards the straight path, and for Thine aid in being grateful to Thee, and in adoring Thee in every good way; and I supplicate Thee for an innocent heart which shall not incline to wickedness and for a true tongue. I supplicate Thee to guide me to all which Thou knowest to be virtuous and to preserve me from all which Thou knowest to be vicious. I supplicate Thee to forgive me my faults for Thou knowest them all.

327. When the Messenger of God entered a place of worship he said, "O God! Pardon my sins, and open for me the

---

[1] This refers to the light of the knowledge of God as opposed to the darkness of ignorance and idolatry.

gates of Thy compassion;" and on leaving he would repeat the same.

328. O Lord, grant to me the love of Thee; grant that I love those that love Thee; grant that I may do the deeds that win Thy love; make Thy love dearer to me than self, family and wealth.

329. O Lord! I make my complaint unto Thee, of my feebleness, the vanity of my efforts. I am insignificant in the sight of men, O Thou Most Merciful! Lord of the weak! Thou art my Lord! Forsake me not. Leave me not a prey to strangers, nor to mine enemies. If Thou art not displeased, I am safe. I seek refuge in the light of Thy countenance, by which all darkness is dispelled, and peace cometh in the Here and the Hereafter. Solve Thou my difficulties as it pleaseth Thee. There is no power, no strength, save in Thee.[1]

Of NEIGHBOURLINESS

330. The best person in God's sight is the best amongst his friends; and the best of neighbours near God is the best person in his own neighbourhood.

331. A Muslim who mixeth with people and putteth up

---

[1] This prayer was uttered by Lord Muhammad in a moment of deep distress. The idolaters of Tā'if had driven him out of the city. The rabble and the slaves followed, hooting and pelting him with stones until the evening. Wounded and bleeding, footsore and weary, he betook himself to prayer.

with their inconveniences, is better than one who doth not mix with them and bear with patience.

332. Do you love your Creator? Love your fellow-beings first.

Of OMENS

333. Of my disciples who will enter Paradise are those who do not use shells (do not consult oracles), and are not influenced by omens, like the people of Ignorance, and who put their whole trust in God.

Of ORPHANS

334. I and the guardian of orphans (whether the orphan be of his near or distant relations, or of strangers) will be in one place in the next world; like my two fingers, nearly touching each other.

335. The best Muslim house is that in which is an orphan, who is benefited; and the worst Muslim house is that in which is an orphan ill-treated.

Of PARENTS

336. (i). Heaven lieth at the feet of Mothers.

336 (ii). God's pleasure is in a father's pleasure; and God's displeasure is in a father's displeasure.

337. He who wisheth to enter Paradise at the best door must please his father and mother.

338. A man is bound to do good to his parents, although they may have injured him.

339. There is no child, a doer of good to his parents, who looketh on them with kindness and affection, but God will grant for every look the rewards for an approved pilgrimage.

Of PEACEMAKING

340. Shall I not inform you of a better act than fasting, alms, and prayers? Making peace between one another: enmity and malice tear up heavenly rewards by the roots.

Of POETRY

341. Some poetry is dressed in knowledge and art.

342. The truest words spoken by any poet are those of Labīd: "Know that everything is vanity save God."

343. God hath treasures beneath the Throne, the key whereof are the tongues of poets.

344. Some poetry containeth much wisdom.

Of POVERTY

345. Poverty is my pride.

346. Poverty may well become a cause of infidelity.

347. O Lord! Keep me alive a poor man, and let me die poor; and raise me amongst the poor.

348. O 'Ā'ishah! Do not turn the poor away, without giving them, if but half a date.

349. Seek for my satisfaction in that of the poor and needy.

350. A man came to Muhammad and said, "Verily I love you." He replied, "Look to what you say." And the man said, "By God! I love you," and repeated the same twice. Lord Muhammad said, "If you are sincere, then prepare yourself for poverty: for poverty reacheth him who loveth me quicker than a torrent reacheth the sea."

Of PRAYER

351. Prayer is the *mi'rāj* (union with, or annihilation in, the Divine Essence by means of continual upward progress) of the Faithful.

352. The Lord doth not regard a prayer in which the heart doth not accompany the body.

353. He whom prayer preventeth not from wrongdoing

and evil, increaseth in naught save in remoteness from the Lord.

354. The key of Paradise is prayer, and the key of prayer is ablution.

355. Say your prayers standing; but if you are not able, sitting; and if unable, on your sides.

Of PRIDE (See also under 'Humility')

356. The proud will not enter Paradise, nor a violent speaker.

357. He will not enter hell, who hath faith equal to a single grain of mustard seed in his heart; and he will not enter Paradise, who hath pride, equal to a single grain of mustard seed, in his heart.

358. Muhammad said: "That person will not enter Paradise who hath one atom of pride in his heart." And a man present said, "Verily, a man is fond of having good clothes, and good shoes." Lord Muhammad said, "God is Beauty and delighteth in the beautiful; but pride is holding man in contempt."

Of PROGRESS

359. Everyone is divinely furthered in accordance with his character.

360. It is your own conduct which will lead you to reward or punishment, as if you had been destined therefor.

361. Every human being hath two inclinations—one prompting him to good and impelling him thereto, and the other prompting him to evil and thereto impelling him; but Divine assistance is nigh, and he who asketh the help of God in contending with the evil promptings of his own heart obtaineth it.

362. The best of good acts in God's sight is that which is constantly attended to although in a small degree.

Of PROPHECIES

363. Verily ye are in an age in which if ye neglect one-tenth of what is ordered, ye will be doomed. After this a time will come, when he who shall observe one-tenth of what is now ordered will be redeemed.

364. Men will be liars towards the end of the world; and will relate such stories as neither you nor your fathers ever heard. Then avoid them, that they may not lead you astray and throw you into contention and strife.

365. The time is near in which nothing will remain of Islām but its name, and of the Kur'ān but its mere appearance, and the mosques of Muslims will be destitute of knowledge and worship; and the learned men will be the worst people under the heavens; and contention and strife will issue from them, and it will return upon themselves.

366. Ye followers of Muhammad, I swear by the Lord, if ye did but know what I know of the future state, verily ye would laugh little and cry much.

367. Verily, of things which I fear for you, after my departure from the world, is this: that the ornaments and goods of the world may be pleasing to you. Then a man said, "O Messenger of God! Doth good bring harm?" Lord Muhammad said, "Verily good doth not bring harm: I mean if there be much wealth, it is a blessing; and there is no harm in it, unless from stinginess and extravagance; like the spring, which causeth nothing to grow but what is good: and harm and destruction are from the abuse thereof."

Of PUNISHMENT

368. God doth not remove anyone out of the world, but that He wisheth to pardon him; and by the diseases of his body and distress for food, He exacteth the punishment of every fault that lieth on his shoulder. (That is, by suffering in this world, he is exempted from punishment in the next.)

369. Verily the reward is as great as the misfortune; that is, the more unfortunate and calamitous one is, the greater and more perfect his reward. And verily, when God loveth a people, He entangleth it in misfortune; therefore, he who is resigned to the pleasure of God, in misfortune, for him is God's favour.

Of PURITY

370. They will enter the Garden of Bliss who have a true, pure and merciful heart.

371. Religion is admonition, and it means being pure.

Of REASON

372. God hath not created anything better than Reason, or anything more perfect, or more beautiful than Reason; the benefits which God giveth are on its account; and understanding is by it, and God's wrath is caused by disregard of it.

Of RELATIVES

373. The best of you, before God and His creation, are those who are best in their own families, and I am the best to my family. When your friend dieth, mention not his vices.

374. He is of the most perfect Muslims, whose disposition is most liked by his own family.

375. The favour of God doth not descend upon that family in which is one who deserts his relations.

376. He is not a perfect performer of the duties of relationship who doeth good to his relatives as they do good to

him. He is perfect who doeth good to his relatives when they do not do good to him.

377. O Messenger of God! Verily I have done a great crime; is there any act by which I may repent? He said, "Have you a mother?" "No," said the questioner. "Have you an aunt?" asked Muhammad. He said, "Yes, I have." Lord Muhammad said, "Go, do good to her, and your crime will be pardoned."

378. The duty of a junior to a senior brother is as that of a child to its father.

379. Giving alms to the poor hath the reward of one alms; but that given to kindred hath two rewards; one, the reward of alms, the other, the reward of helping relations.

380. A man's first charity should be to his own family, if poor.

Of REPENTANCE

381. A sincere repenter of faults is like him who hath committed none.

Of REVERENCE

382. Muhammad said one day to his companions, "Reverence God as becometh you." They said, "Verily, O Apostle of God, we do reverence Him, and praise be to God who

hath imbued us with it." Then Muhammad said, "It is not so; but whoever reverenceth God as it is suitable for him to do must guard his head from humbling itself to others, and from pride and arrogance towards God and God's creatures; he must guard his senses from whatever is wrong, and must guard his mouth from eating forbidden things, and his heart from receiving what is prohibited; and he must keep death in mind, and the rotting of his bones. And whoever wisheth for future rewards must abandon the ornaments of the world. Therefore, anyone attending to the aforementioned points has verily reverenced God as it is his duty to do."

Of RICHES

383. Riches are not from abundance of worldly goods, but from a contented mind.

384. It is difficult, for a man laden with riches, to climb the steep path that leadeth to bliss.

385. Whoever desireth the world and its riches, in a lawful manner, in order to withhold himself from begging, and for a livelihood for his family, and for being kind to his neighbour, will come to God with his face bright as the full moon on the fourteenth night of the lunar month.

386. Wealth, properly employed, is a blessing; and a man may lawfully endeavour to increase it by honest means.

Of SEEMLINESS

387. A Bedouin was standing in the mosque of the Prophet, and defiled it; when he was immediately taken hold of; and Muhammad said, "Let him alone, and throw a skin of water upon the spot; because ye were not created but as comforters and not sent to create hardships." And they let him alone till he had done, and then Muhammad called the Bedouin to him, and said, "This mosque is not a proper place for that, or any kind of filth; mosques are only for the mention of God, saying prayers, and reading the Kur'ān."

Of SELF-INDULGENCE

388. Muhammad asked his companions, "What are your opinions of the merits of that person, who drinketh liquor, committeth adultery, and stealeth? What should his punishment be?" They said, "God and His Messenger know best." He said, "These are great sins, and the punishment for them very dire." (This question was asked before the precepts in the Kur'ān, in which those things are forbidden, descended.)

Of SERVANTS

389. To those of your servants who please you give to eat what you eat yourself; and clothe them as yourself; but those who do not please you, part with them; and punish not God's creatures.

390. He will not enter Paradise who behaveth ill to his slaves. The companions said, "O Apostle of God! Have you not told us, that there will be a great many slaves and orphans amongst your disciples?" He said, "Yes; then be kind to them as to your own children, and give them to eat of what you eat yourselves. The slaves that say their prayers are your brothers."

391. Zaid, Muhammad's servant, said, "I served Muhammad ten years, and he never said 'Uff'[1] to me; and never said, 'Why did you do so?' and never said, 'Why did you not do so?' "

Of THE SICK

392. There is not any Muslim who visiteth another in sickness, in the forenoon, but that seventy thousand angels send blessings upon him till the evening; and there is no one who visiteth the sick, in the afternoon, but that seventy thousand angels send blessings upon him till daybreak, and there will be a pardon for him in Paradise.

393. Feed the hungry and visit the sick, and free the captive, if he be unjustly confined. Assist any person oppressed, whether Muslim or non-Muslim.

394. Whoever visiteth a sick person, an angel calleth from heaven, "Be happy in the world, and happy be your walking, and take you a habitation in Paradise."

[1] An exclamation expressive of displeasure.

395. Whoever visiteth a sick person always entereth into and swims in a sea of mercy until he sitteth down; and when he sitteth, he is drowned therein.

396. When you go to visit the sick, comfort his grief, and say, "You will get well and live long," because although this saying will not prevent what is predestined, it will solace his soul.

397. Verily God will say on the Day of Judgment, "O children of Adam! I was sick and ye did not visit Me." And the sons of Adam will say, "O our defender, how could we visit Thee? For Thou art the Lord of the Universe, and art free from sickness." And God will say, "O men! Such a one was sick and you did not visit him." And God will say, "O children of Adam, I asked you for food, and ye gave it Me not?" And the children of Adam will say, "O our patron, how could we give Thee food, seeing Thou art the cherisher of the Universe, and art free from hunger and eating?" And God will say, "Such a one asked you for bread and you did not give it him."

Of SILENCE

398. Much silence and a good disposition, there are no two works better than those.

Of SIN

399. Can any one walk through water without wetting his feet? The companions replied, "No"; Muhammad said,

"Such is the condition of those of the world; they are not safe from sins."

Of TRUTH

400. He is not of me who, when he speaketh, speaketh falsely; who, when he promiseth, breaketh his promises; and who, when trust is reposed in him, faileth in his trust.

401. No man is true in the truest sense of the word but he who is true in word, in deed, and in thought.

402. Strive always to excel in virtue and truth.

403. It is not worthy of a speaker of truth to curse people.

404. Appropriate to yourselves the truth. Avoid lying.

405. Say what is true, although it may be bitter and displeasing to people.

Of UNDERSTANDING

406. It is not a sixth or a tenth of a man's devotion which is acceptable to God, but only such portions thereof as he offereth with understanding and true devotional spirit.

407. Verily, a man hath performed prayers, fasts, charity, pilgrimage and all other good works; but he will not be rewarded except by the proportion of his understanding.

Of USURY

408. The taker of usury and the giver of it, and the writer of its papers and the witness to it, are equal in crime.

Of WIDOWS

409. A giver of maintenance to widows and the poor, is like a bestower in the way of God, an utterer of prayers all the night, and a keeper of constant fast.

410. I and a woman whose colour and cheeks shall have become black from toiling in the sun shall be near to one another in the next world as my two fingers; and that is a handsome widow, whose colour and cheeks shall have become black in bringing up her family.

Of WIVES

411. Admonish your wives with kindness.

412. A Muslim must not hate his wife; and if he be displeased with one bad quality in her, then let him be pleased with another which is good.

413. Do you beat your own wife as you would a slave? That must you not do.

414. I (Mu'avīyah b. Ḥaidah) said, "O Apostle of God! What is my duty to my wife?" He said, "That you give her

to eat as you eat yourself, and clothe her as you clothe yourself; and do not slap her in the face nor abuse her, nor separate yourself from her in displeasure."

415. Give your wife good counsel; and if she has goodness in her, she will soon take it, and leave off idle talking;
and do not beat your noble wife like a slave.

416. Muhammad said: "Beat not your wives." Then Omar
came to the Rasūl (Muhammad) and said, "Wives have got
the upper hand of their husbands from hearing this."

417. He is the most perfect Muslim whose disposition is
best; and the best of you are they who behave best to their
wives.

418. A virtuous wife is a man's best treasure.

Of WOMEN

419. Women are the twin-halves of men.

420. The world and all things in it are valuable; but the
most valuable thing in the world is a virtuous woman.

421. The best women are the virtuous; they are the most
affectionate to infants, and the most careful of their husbands' property.

422. When a woman performeth the five times of prayer,
and fasteth the month of Ramadān, and is chaste, and is not

disobedient to her husband, then tell her to enter Paradise by whichever door she liketh.

423. Verily a great number of women are assembled near my family, complaining of their husbands; and those men who ill-treat their wives do not behave well. He is not of my way who teacheth a woman to stray.

424. Asmā, daughter of Yazīd, said, "Victuals were brought to Muhammad, and he put them before some of us women who were present, and said, 'Eat ye.' But notwithstanding we were hungry we said, 'We have no inclination.' Muhammad said, 'O women! Do not mix hunger with lies.' "

425. Whoever doeth good to girls, it will be a curtain to him from hell-fire.

426. Whoever befriendeth two girls till they come of age, will be in the next world along with me, like my two fingers joining each other.

427. Whoever befriendeth three daughters, or three sisters, and teacheth them manners, and is affectionate to them, till they come of age, may God apportion Paradise for him.

428. Whoever hath a daughter, and doth not bury her alive, or scold her, or prefer his male children to her, may God bring him into Paradise.[1]

---

[1] This refers to the practice of female infanticide which Muhammad abolished.

429. Shall I not point out to you the best of virtues? It is your doing good to your daughter when she is returned to you having been divorced by her husband.

430. God enjoins you to treat women well, for they are your mothers, daughters, and aunts.

431. The rights of women are sacred. See that women are maintained in the rights assigned to them.

432. Do not prevent your women from coming to the mosque.

Of THE WORLD

433. The love of the world is the root of all evil.

434. This world is a prison for the Faithful, but a Paradise for unbelievers.

435. The world is a magician greater than Hārūt and Mārūt, and you should avoid it.

436. The world is sweet in the heart, and green to the eye; and verily God hath brought you, after those that went before you: then look to your actions, and abstain from the world and its wickedness.

437. The world is as a prison and as a famine to Muslims; and when they leave it you may say they leave famine and a prison.

438. Be in the world like a traveller, or like a passer-on, and reckon yourself as of the dead.

439. Cursed is this world and cursed is all that is in this world, except the remembrance of God and that which aideth thereto.

GLOSSARY

BELIEVER.—One who accepts the Revelation of the Kur'ān, a Muslim

COMPANIONS.—The immediate disciples of Muhammad.

DĀR-AL-ISLĀM.—The Home of Islam, Muslimdom.

FIRE.—Hell.

FRIENDS.—The 'companions'.

GARDEN.—Heaven.

HIJRAH.—Lit. 'migration'. (1) Departure of Muhammad from Mecca to Medina. (2) The Muslim era. (3) A Muslim's leaving a country under non-Muslim rule. (4) Fleeing from sin.—The Hijra took place on the 4th of Rabi 'I, 2nd July, 622; but the Caliph Omar, who instituted the official Muslim era, naming it after this event, dated it from the first day of the first lunar month of that year, Moharrum, equivalent to 28th April, 622.

IGNORANCE.—The 'Dark Age' of Arabian history, the period preceding the advent of Muhammad.

IMĀN.—Faith.

MU'MIN.—Faithful, a Muslim.

MUSLIM.—A believer in Islām, a 'Mahometan'.

PEOPLE OF THE BOOK.—Believers in a revealed moral religion, Jews, Christians, Ṣābians, etc.

RASŪL.—Apostle, Messenger of God, a Man sent of God, a prophet.

SUNNAH OR HADITH.—The recorded traditions of the everyday actions and of the words which fell from the lips of the Prophet during the twenty-three years of his ministry. These are classed as 'authentic' only if an unbroken chain of absolutely reliable narrators can be established going back to one of the chief companions of the Prophet. The task of collecting these traditions was undertaken within eleven years of the death of the Prophet. They must not be confused with the Kur'ān, which is the revealed Word of God (see below).

SURAH.—'A row or series.' A term used for the 'chapters' of the Kur'ān, of which there are 114.

WORD OF GOD.—al-Kur'ān, the Koran. Revealed through the Prophet Muhammad. A physical change came over the Prophet, like one in a trance, each time he received a revelation. These utterances were written down immediately by the Companions on any available writing material. The written pieces were distributed among the Muslims and many committed them to memory. Under the directions of the Prophet himself, the chapters and verses were arranged by the scribes according to significance and not in chronological order. Each *Sura* (chapter) was given a distinctive heading and contains a varying number of *Ayats* (verses), and they are thus of very unequal size. Muhammad used to make reference to chapter and verse whenever he quoted the Kur'ān or asked a reciter to do so. Soon after the death of the Prophet, many of the reciters of the Kur'ān were killed during the battle of Yemama, and in order to safeguard against any possibility of the Kur'ān being lost, Abu Bakr, the first Caliph (successor of Muhammad), ordered the written pieces to be collected together and kept in a chest. This was done in less than two years after the death of the Prophet, under the supervision of Zaid-bin-Sabit, Muhammad's amanuensis, and a person of high integrity. Under the orders of Othman, the third Caliph, all the copies of the Kur'ān dispersed throughout the Islamic world were recalled and burned. From the authoritative collection of Abu Bakr, copies of the Kur'ān were transcribed and Othman employed the same Zaid son of Sabit and other reliable scribes to do this work. Othman, with the help of twelve persons, with Ali at their head, all of whom knew the whole of the Kur'ān by heart, supervised and tested the accuracy of the transcriptions as the work was proceeding. These authentic volumes, with the seal and signature of Othman, were distributed within eleven years of the death of the Prophet, to such distant lands as Iraq, Persia, Syria, Palestine and Egypt. Thanks to the care of the early Muslims, every copy of the Kur'ān today is exactly word for word as it was uttered by the Prophet.

Bibliography

AMEER ALI, *The Spirit of Islām.*

AMEER ALI, *The Ethics of Islām.*

ARNOLD, SIR EDWIN, *Pearls of the Faith.*

ARNOLD, T. W., *The Preaching of Islām.*

LANE-POOLE, S., *Studies in a Mosque.*

SMITH, R. BOSWORTH, *Mohammad and Mohammadanism.*

THOMAS, BERTRAM, *The Arabs.*

Note No.   *Chapter and Verse.*

2, 5.   xlii. 13: 'God has opened to you the Way of Religion
which He commended to Noah that he might follow
in it. It is the same Faith which we have revealed to
thee, and which we showed to Abraham, to Moses,
and to Jesus, to the end that true Religion might continue in the earth. Divide not yourselves into sects.'

2, 6.   ii. 136: 'Say: We believe in God and that which is revealed unto us, and that which was revealed unto
Abraham, and Ishmael, and Isaac and Jacob, and that
which Moses and Jesus received, and that which the
Prophets received from their Lord. We make no distinction between any of them.'

3.   xxxv. 24: 'There has never been a nation to whom God
has not sent a Prophet.'

4.   xiii. 38: 'To every age its own Book.'

7.   iv. 171: 'O People of the Scripture! Do not exaggerate
in your religion nor utter aught concerning God save
the truth. The Messiah, Jesus son of Mary, was only a
messenger of God, and His word which He conveyed
unto Mary, a spirit from Him (God). So believe in
God and His messengers, and say not "Three"—
Cease! (It is) better for you! —God is only One God.
Far is it removed from His transcendent majesty that

He should have a son. His is all that is in the heavens and all that is in the earth.'

9.   ii. 255: 'God, there is no God but Him, the Living, the Self-Subsisting, the Eternal. Neither slumber nor sleep overtaketh Him. Unto Him belongeth whatsoever is in the heavens and whatsoever is in the earth. . . . He knoweth that which is in front of them (His creatures) and that which is behind them, while they encompass nothing of His Knowledge save what He wills. His Throne includeth the heavens and the earth, and He is never weary and fatigued of guarding and preserving them. He is the Sublime and the Supreme in Glory.'

ii. 163: 'And your God is one God, there is no God but He; Loving, Gracious, most Merciful.'

10.   v. 39: 'Whosoever repenteth sincerely after his wrong-doing and amendeth, God will relent towards him.'

xxxix. 53: 'Despair not of the mercy of God, who forgiveth all sins. He is the Forgiving, the Merciful.'

14.   ii. 256: 'There is no compulsion in religion. Truth stands out clear from error; and he who rejecteth false deities and believeth in God hath grasped a firm handhold which will never break.'

16.   xvii. 31: 'Slay not your children, fearing a fall to poverty. We shall provide for them and for you. Behold, the slaying of them is a great sin.'

xvi. 58–9: 'When if one of them receiveth tidings of the birth of a female, his face remaineth darkened, and he is wroth inwardly. He hideth himself from the folk because of the evil of that whereof he hath had tidings (asking himself): Shall he keep it in contempt or bury it beneath the dust. Verily, evil is their judgment.'

17.   iv. 3: 'Ye may marry of the women who seem good to

you, two or three or four; but if ye fear that ye cannot observe equity between them, then espouse but a single wife.'

iv. 129: 'And ye will never be able to be equitable and just between women no matter how much ye may strive to do so.

18. xvi. 97: 'Whosoever doeth right, whether male or female, him verily We shall quicken with good life, and recompense.'

ii. 228: 'And they (women) have rights similar to those (of men), over them in kindness and men are a degree above them.'

19. iv. 7: 'Unto the men (of a family) belongeth a share of that which parents and near kindred leave, and unto the women a share of that which parents and near kindred leave, whether it be little or much—a legal share.'

22. ABLUTION, *AL-WODHU'* (Physical Cleanliness). Obligatory before Prayers (Spiritual Purification).

1. Begin by saying "In the name of God, the Merciful, the Compassionate".

2. Wash the hands up to the wrist, once, twice or thrice, according to the quantity of water available, beginning with the right hand.

3. Rinse out the mouth and gargle the throat thrice.

4. Clean the nostrils by sniffing water into each nostril thrice.

5. Wash the face from the forehead to the chin and from ear to ear thrice.

6. Wash the forearms up to the elbow thrice, beginning with the right.

7. Pass the wet hands over the head, cleaning the hair from the forehead to the back of the neck thrice.

8. Clean the ears with the tips of the fingers thrice.

9. Pass the wet hands right round the neck, cleaning it thrice.

10. Finally, wash the feet up to the ankles thrice, first the right and then the left.

The Muslim Prayer[1]

It is a simple dignified form of worship following a set formula of postures and devotions (petitions and responses faintly suggesting an unintoned Litany in the English Church Service). The worshippers do not bare their heads, they remove their shoes or sandals, perform certain ritualistic ablutions, and then assemble to form a long line facing Mecca (the Ka'ba), the leader taking up a position a little to the front of them in the centre.

Posture 1.—They stand in a reverent way, with the palms of their hands raised to the ears.

Affirmations and prayers in a low reverent voice.

"God is greater than all else."

Posture 2.—Still standing, the arms are lowered and the right hand placed over the left one.

"Glory and praise to Thee, O God ! Blessed is Thy name and exalted is Thy Majesty. There is no one worthy of worship and service but Thee. In the Name of God, the Merciful, the

[1] From *The Arabs,* by Bertram Thomas.

Compassionate. Praise be to God the Lord of the Worlds, the Merciful, the Compassionate, the Master of the Day of Judgment. Thee, O God, Thee only do we worship, and Thee only do we beseech for help. Guide us into the right path, the path of those Thou hast blest, not of those with whom Thou art displeased, nor of those who have gone astray." Amen.

The worshipper then recites a portion of the Kur'ān he has committed to memory, e.g.—

"Say: 'Verily my prayers and my worship, my life and my death are unto God, the Lord of the Worlds. No associate has He. Thus have I been commanded and I am the first to surrender myself unto Him.'"
"God is greater than all else."

Posture 3.—Bodies are bent forward at right angles, the hands are lowered and placed on the knees.

"Glory to my Lord, the Exalted." (Repeated thrice.)

Posture 4.—The standing position is resumed.

"God accepts him who is grateful to Him.
O our Lord ! All praise be to Thee.
God is greater than all else."

Posture 5.—The worshippers next kneel down, their bodies bowed over, supported with the hands on the ground, palms downwards, their heads bowed reverently, so that their brows touch the ground.

"Glory to my Lord, the Most High." (Repeated thrice.)

A bow that is repeated once more, with the same words and ending

"God is greater than all else."

Posture 6.—A sitting-kneeling position follows with the hands resting on the knees.

"Glory to my Lord, the Most Exalted." (Repeated thrice.)
"God is greater than all else."

This concludes the first phase of the devotions, and is called a Rakat. Prayers are some of two, some of three, some of four Rakats. To end with, a prayer is said for the Prophets, the Faithful, and for the worshippers in some such form as the following:

"Homage be to God and all sincere worship is unto Him.
"Peace and the mercy of God and His blessings be upon thee, O Prophet! Peace be upon us and all righteous servants of God.
"I bear witness that there is but one God and that Muhammad is His servant and His messenger.
"May it please Thee, O God, to be gracious to Muhammad and the followers of Muhammad as Thou wast gracious to Abraham and the followers of Abraham and to bless Muhammad and the followers of Muhammad as Thou didst bless Abraham and the followers of Abraham, for surely Thou art Praised and Magnified."

This is usually followed by:

"O Lord! Grant that I may always observe my prayers and that my offspring may do so also, and accept, O our Lord, this suppli-

cation of mine. Our Lord! Forgive me and forgive my parents and all believers on the day of reckoning."

And finally the worshippers turn their heads to right and left with the greeting—

"Peace be with you, and the mercy of Allah."